THE
ANTI-PROCESSED
AIR FRYER
COOKBOOK

THE ANTI-PROCESSED AIR FRYER COOKBOOK

Ditch ultra-processed foods with these 90 speedy recipes

HEATHER THOMAS

HarperCollins*Publishers*

CONTENTS

INTRODUCTION

Owning an air fryer can transform your life. It will not only save you time, energy and money but it's also convenient, accessible and a healthy way to cook delicious food, using less fat and oil than more conventional methods. You can cook many of your favourite meals in an air fryer in minutes, making it perfect for quick breakfasts and speedy suppers. What's more, it's easy to use and to clean. Most air fryers have a digital touch screen so all you have to do is set the temperature and cooking time and away you go.

WHAT IS AN AIR FRYER?

An air fryer is essentially a mini convection oven fitted with a powerful fan and a heating element. It blows hot air over the food to be cooked, and almost anything that you would usually bake, grill (broil), shallow- or deep-fry can be cooked in an air fryer in less time and at a lower temperature. Whether you're cooking a whole roast chicken for a family lunch, some marinated salmon fillets, French fries, grilled halloumi or even chocolate brownies, you will be amazed at the results. Chicken is golden brown and crispy on the outside but deliciously moist and tender when you bite into it. Chips and roast potatoes are appetizingly golden and crunchy outside while staying soft and succulent inside.

HEALTHY FOOD

We all want to be fit, enjoy good health and eat nutritious food. However, many everyday foods sold in supermarkets contain a cocktail of human-made chemicals. Even some foods labelled as healthy are in fact ultra-processed foods (UPF) which means they are nothing of the sort. If you read the list of ingredients on the packet of your favourite biscuits, crisps, ice cream, breakfast cereal, mayo or even oat milk, you probably wouldn't recognize most of them and you would be right to feel confused or even alarmed. We enjoy the sweet, spicy and salty flavours of these products and love the fact that many are convenient, which means we don't have to spend time preparing and cooking meals from scratch. But nutritionally and health-wise, these foods may be harmful.

WHAT IS UPF?

An ultra-processed food is one that has been industrially produced and altered from its original form to create an edible food-like substance – it is not 'real' food. Most UPF is aggressively marketed, attractively packaged and often cheaper and more convenient to eat than unprocessed food. You may be surprised to know that some mass-produced wholemeal bread, 'healthy' granola and flapjacks, cooked ham, salad dressings, prepacked sandwiches, pesto sauces, sausages and even fruit yoghurts lining supermarket shelves may qualify as UPF.

Eating ultra-processed food on a regular basis can have an adverse effect on our health, especially in the long term. Many scientists and doctors believe that a diet high in UPF could be contributing to global obesity. These foods tend to contain few nutrients and cause inflammation in the body because they contain a lot of fat and carbohydrates, so eating them makes us more likely to suffer from chronic diseases. These include cardiovascular disease, cancer, type 2 diabetes, high blood pressure, dementia and depression. They may also shorten our lives as well as affecting our gut health. The soft (or dry) textures and strong flavours of these foods can be addictive and may lead us to overeat, gain weight and reduce the protein and fibre in our diet. This issue goes right to the heart of our health and wellbeing.

RECOGNIZING UPF

How do you recognize UPF? If it's wrapped in plastic and it contains at least one ingredient that you would not find in your kitchen at home, it may be a UPF. These foods often have high levels of saturated fat, oil, sugar and salt, plus several additives. Read the labels and look out for the following clues:

- artificial flavourings
- artificial colourings
- emulsifiers
- modified starches
- gums

- thickeners
- hydrolyzed protein
- glutamates, such as monosodium glutamate

- invert sugar
- humectants
- stabilizers
- artificial sweeteners

THE NOVA SCALE

The NOVA scale divides food and food products into four groups according to how processed they are. If you want to avoid or minimize your intake of processed foods, you need to aim to eat the foods within groups 1 and 2 below.

GROUP 1: UNPROCESSED OR MINIMALLY PROCESSED FOODS

Dishes cooked at home or in restaurants with unprocessed or minimally processed ingredients (e.g. ingredients which have been frozen, pasteurized, vacuum-packed, ground, dried or crushed).
This group includes fresh meat, fish, eggs, milk, vegetables, nuts, raw pulses, frozen or dried fruit and vegetables, fermented plain yoghurt.

GROUP 2: PROCESSED COOKING INGREDIENTS

Ingredients which are usually derived from group 1 foods through drying, crushing, grinding, refining, and so on.
This group includes salt, oils, vinegar, honey, butter, brown or white sugar.

GROUP 3: PROCESSED FOODS THAT COMBINE GROUPS 1 AND 2 FOODS

These foods are often smoked, cured, preserved or baked.
This group includes jam, chutney, pickled or bottled vegetables, tinned beans, tinned fish, cheese, homemade bread, smoked salmon or trout.

GROUP 4: ULTRA-PROCESSED FOODS AND DRINKS PRODUCTS

This includes heavily processed foods that contain additives to flavour, colour, sweeten and emulsify and extend their shelf life; processed raw materials, such as modified starches; and ingredients of industrial origin.
This group includes most baked products and breakfast cereals, cereal and muesli bars, carbonated sweet drinks, most fruit-flavoured yoghurts and ice creams, many vegan foods, processed meats such as hot dogs, ham, salami, sausages and chicken nuggets, mass-produced sliced bread, cakes, doughnuts, muffins, cookies and takeaway sandwiches, many salty snacks, crisps (potato chips), sweets (candy), instant soups, processed cheese slices, frozen pizza, pasta sauces, mayonnaise and oat milk.
Check the labels on all group 4 foods before buying them. Some foods labelled as healthy, natural, high-protein, low-sugar or low-fat may be ultra-processed.

HOW TO AVOID UPF

1. Choose unprocessed foods in their original state.
2. Eat a plant-rich diet which includes lots of vegetables, pulses, fungi, nuts, wholegrains and fruit.
3. Avoid food products with a long list of ingredients on the label.
4. Cook from scratch whenever possible, so you know exactly what you are eating and can control the quality.
5. Make your own packed lunches and snack foods.
6. Snack on wholefoods such as fruit, vegetables, nuts, Greek yoghurt, and so on.
7. Avoid processed foods that contain ingredients you don't recognize or you do not have in your kitchen at home.
8. Practise simple swaps, for example:
   - eat plain yoghurt with fresh fruit, seeds and nuts rather than fruit-flavoured yoghurt;
   - make porridge with whole oats instead of eating processed breakfast cereal;
   - buy a fresh sourdough loaf rather than a supermarket sliced one;
   - make your own salad dressings, mayonnaise and pasta sauces.

HOW UPF AFFECTS APPETITE AND CALORIE INTAKE

Research and clinical trials show that if your diet includes a lot of ultra-processed foods you eat about 500 calories more per day than people who eat unprocessed and minimally processed foods. You are also likely to have higher levels of an appetite-stimulating hormone and lower levels of a hormone that suppresses appetite. These hormone levels may make you feel hungry more often, or mean that you eat larger meals and more high-calorie snacks. Researchers have also found that many people who eat a lot of UPF foods often replace home-cooked meals made with fresh ingredients with multiple snacks.

If you can reduce the UPF you eat, choose healthier snacks and cook more nutritious meals from scratch, your gut microbiome will be healthier. You will also live longer and your diet will mean you're less likely to suffer from cardiovascular disease, type 2 diabetes or become obese. There is evidence of a link between diets high in UPF and body mass index (BMI); people who eat more UPF are increasingly likely to be overweight or clinically obese.

HOW TO USE THIS BOOK

Switching to an anti-processed diet can feel like quite a big undertaking when there's so much information out there, and so many pantry and fridge staples seem as though they're suddenly off the table. This book aims to simplify the process; in fact, many of the recipes include favourite items that you might have been told should be avoided completely.

The reality is that eating an anti-processed diet is a lot about recognizing ingredients on food labels and knowing what to avoid. The beauty of this is that to switch your diet to a healthier one, you don't necessarily need to completely cut out condiments or packaged foods. It simply means you need to find options you enjoy that are low in trans fats, sugar and salt.

When assessing labels, there are a few things to be aware of. Trans fats are usually listed as 'hydrogenated fat' or 'partially hydrogenated vegetable oil'; high-sugar foods will contain more than 22.5g total sugar per 100g; high-sodium foods will contain more than 1.5g sodium per 100g; and foods high in saturated fats will have more than 5g per 100g. While these markers don't always mean something is ultra-processed, it is still worth avoiding foods in these categories due to their unhealthy nature.

A good rule of thumb is to be aware of ingredients that you don't recognize or don't sound like food, such as high-fructose corn syrup and hydrolysed proteins, additives, flavour enhancers, artificial colours, sweeteners and thickeners, and anti-foaming, bulking, carbonating, foaming, gelling and glazing agents. If you don't think you could recreate the food item at home based on the ingredient list, it's a sign that the food is likely to be ultra-processed.

Within this book, you'll find that there are ingredients that can be ultra-processed depending upon the supplier or producer. This includes things like: white bread, tomato ketchup and other sauces, bacon and sausages. In these cases, we've used fresh white bread from a bakery, good-quality and premium sausages and bacon from butchers (who use natural casings and no additives) and organic ketchup and condiments. This way, you can still enjoy your favourite delicious meals, while still avoiding UPFs!

USING YOUR AIR FRYER

An air fryer is an incredibly useful addition to any kitchen, and you'll soon wonder how you survived without one. It won't take up much space on the kitchen counter and is very easy to use. Before you start cooking, make sure you read the manual and familiarize yourself with the controls. Air fryers vary considerably depending on the manufacturer and model, and temperatures and cooking times may also vary depending on the size and capacity of the air fryer. Don't worry about this – the more you use your air fryer, the better you'll get to know it and the easier it will be to make any necessary adjustments.

GUIDELINES

1   Most air fryers need to be preheated before you use them, so check whether yours has a button for preheating. Also, read your manual to find out the recommended preheating time – it's usually 5 minutes maximum.

2   You can set the timer for the maximum cooking time and check or flip the food halfway through (if recommended), and also check it regularly at short intervals, such as every 2 or 5 minutes. To look at and check the food you're cooking just remove the basket. The air fryer will turn off automatically when you do this, and then turn on again when you replace the basket.

3   When you're cooking meat, poultry and fish, you can check whether it's cooked through by inserting a knife and cutting it open. If you want to be sure your food is perfectly cooked, err on the side of caution and use a digital meat thermometer with a temperature probe (always insert into the thickest part of the food). This ensures that you'll get the best results and that food is fully cooked and safe to eat. Look for these readings:

- **Fish: 63°C/145°F**
- **Chicken and other poultry: 74°C/165°F**
- **Lamb: 63°C/145°F minimum – higher if you like it well cooked**
- **Beef: 63°C/145°F minimum – higher if you like it well cooked**
- **Pork: 63°C/145°F minimum.**
- **Sausages: 74°C/165°F**

4   Unless a recipe specifies otherwise, only spray food to be cooked lightly with oil. If you don't have a spray bottle, you can use a pastry brush.

5   Don't use highly processed seed oils or palm oil. Use a minimally processed healthy oil with a high smoke point, such as avocado oil or an extra light olive oil. These oils can withstand higher temperatures without burning and smoking. The smoke point of the oil is very important and that's why avocado oil or a light olive oil is recommended. You only use 2–3 squirts of oil so a small amount goes a very long way – unlike when you use oil for shallow- and deep-frying or roasting.

6   When preparing food for the air fryer, follow these simple rules:

- Cut the food into similar-sized pieces so they cook evenly.

- Pat dry any moist foods, such as potatoes or fish fillets, with kitchen paper (paper towels) before air frying to make them more crisp.

- Do not overcrowd your air fryer – always cook food in a single layer (unless directed otherwise) with space around each item so that the air can flow around it. You may have to cook the food in batches, depending on the size of your air fryer.

7   When cooking food in the air fryer, follow these simple rules:

- For smaller items such as fries, shake the basket once every 5 minutes or so to help them cook evenly and become crisp and crunchy.

- Turn over or flip breaded chicken pieces, prawns (shrimp) and vegetables halfway through the cooking time, so they brown and crisp evenly on both sides.

- You can line the air fryer basket with baking parchment, kitchen foil or a silicone liner. Again, check the manual to ensure that these are safe to use in your machine.

SEASONINGS

Before cooking meat, fish, poultry and vegetables in the air fryer, season them with salt and pepper plus any dried herbs, ground spices, dry rubs and marinades you like. There are suggestions for these in the recipes.

CLEANING THE AIR FRYER

Always wash the air fryer drawer or basket after using it. Leave it to cool after cooking and then wash it by hand in soapy water before drying and replacing it. Be gentle and don't use harsh scourers which may damage the lining of the basket. Check the manual to find out whether it's dishwasher safe.

SAFETY

- Always wear oven gloves when removing hot food from the air fryer.
- Stand the air fryer on an even surface and don't push it back against the wall. You need to leave room for air to circulate around the sides and over the top.
- Check food you are cooking frequently to ensure that it does not burn or become charred.

EQUIPMENT

You don't need many utensils or much special equipment for cooking with an air fryer. However, you might find the following useful:

- meat thermometer (see page 13)
- spray bottle for oil
- pastry brush for oiling or brushing over marinades and glazes
- air fryer liners
- an ovenproof baking dish that fits inside the basket
- baking trays or cake tins (pans) that fit inside the basket; for small air fryers you'll probably need a 15 x 15cm (6 x 6in) tin
- a grill rack, pizza pan and muffin tin (pan) that fit inside the basket.

BREAKFASTS & BRUNCHES

You can make breakfast and brunch the main event using these quick and easy air fryer recipes. Choose tasty meals cooked in the air fryer with just a little oil or butter and make greasy fry-ups a thing of the past. Rather than buying a ready meal at the supermarket, try cooking these family favourites at home. There's a wide range of sweet and savoury breakfast recipes in this chapter, from hash browns to corn fritters and granola. These recipes will allow you to enhance every flavour without adding a single additive!

FRENCH TOAST FINGERS

French toast has never been easier, and this gently spiced version is so delicious.
If you don't eat dairy, you can use plant milk in the batter, and serve it with non-dairy
coconut yoghurt.

SERVES: 3-4 / PREP: 10 MINUTES / COOK: 4-6 MINUTES

spray oil (see tip)
2 large free-range eggs
60ml (2fl oz/¼ cup) milk
a few drops of vanilla extract
a good pinch of ground
    cinnamon
4 thick slices of day-old white
    bread
sea salt and freshly ground
    black pepper

TO SERVE
maple syrup, for drizzling
soft cheese or Greek yoghurt
blueberries, for sprinkling

1 Heat the air fryer to 190°C/375°F. If your basket is not non-stick, line it with baking parchment and spray it lightly with oil.

2 Put the eggs, milk, vanilla extract and cinnamon in a bowl and whisk them until they are well combined. Season lightly with salt and pepper.

3 Cut each slice of bread into 3 fingers and soak them briefly in the beaten egg mixture. Don't leave them for too long or they will become soggy and fall apart.

4 Arrange the bread fingers in the air fryer in a single layer so they don't touch each other. You may have to cook them in two batches depending on the size of your air fryer. Cook the fingers for 4–6 minutes, or until they are cooked through and golden brown – turn them once if you like.

5 Serve the toast fingers hot, drizzled with maple syrup, with some soft cheese or yoghurt and blueberries on the side.

★ Tip: Use avocado or light olive oil, which both have a high smoke point. You can buy them in spray form or decant them into a small spray bottle to keep on the kitchen counter. You only need 2–3 squirts for most food items. See also page 14.

VARIATIONS
• Use brioche or try wholemeal bread.
• Beat a little melted butter into the egg mixture.
• Lightly dust the French toast with icing (confectioner's) sugar.
• Serve with sliced banana, strawberries or even crispy bacon.

CORN FRITTERS WITH CHILLI DRIZZLE

These delicious fritters are perfect for breakfast, lunch or snacks and appetizers. Cooking them in the air fryer uses far less oil than the traditional method of frying them in a pan.

SERVES 3-4 / PREP: 15 MINUTES / COOK: 13-15 MINUTES

115g (4oz/scant 1 cup)
    self-raising (self-rising) flour
2 medium free-range eggs
1-2 tbsp milk
200g (7oz/1 cup) tinned
    sweetcorn kernels, drained
a good pinch of chilli powder
3 spring onions (scallions),
    finely chopped
a few sprigs of parsley, finely
    chopped
spray oil
sweet chilli sauce, for drizzling
sea salt and freshly ground
    black pepper

SMASHED AVOCADO

1 large ripe avocado, peeled
    and stoned (pitted)
1 garlic clove, crushed
a pinch of crushed chilli flakes
juice of ½ lime or lemon

1   Make the smashed avocado: mash the avocado with a fork in a bowl until it has a chunky consistency. Stir in the garlic and a few chilli flakes, and then add a little lemon or lime juice to taste. Cover the bowl and set it aside while you make the fritters.

2   Sift the flour, salt and pepper into a bowl and make a well in the centre. Whisk the eggs and milk in a separate bowl and then stir into the seasoned flour. The batter should be slightly wet but relatively stiff – if necessary, add more flour or milk.

3   Gently stir in the sweetcorn, chilli powder, spring onions and parsley, taking care not to overmix. Take spoonfuls of the mixture and flatten them with a spatula.

4   Heat the air fryer to 180°C/350°F.

5   Line the air fryer basket with baking parchment and spray it lightly with oil. Add the fritters in a single layer, taking care not to overcrowd them – if necessary, cook them in two batches. Cook the fritters for 7 minutes, then spray them lightly with oil and turn them over. Cook them for a further 6–8 minutes until they are golden brown and crisp.

6   Serve immediately, drizzled with chilli sauce, with the smashed avocado.

BREAKFAST FRITTATA

A savoury breakfast packed with protein and vegetables will set you up for the day and this frittata does just that. What's more, it's very versatile and great for using up leftovers. Vegetarians can leave out the ham.

SERVES 3-4 /PREP: 10 MINUTES / COOK: 12-16 MINUTES

spray oil
4 medium free-range eggs
60ml (2fl oz/¼ cup) double (heavy) cream
50g (2oz/½ cup) coarsely grated cheese, e.g. Cheddar or Parmesan
50g (2oz/⅓ cup) diced cooked ham
4 button mushrooms, thinly sliced
4 cherry tomatoes, quartered
2 spring onions (scallions), sliced
2 tbsp chopped parsley or chives
salt and freshly ground black pepper

1   Heat the air fryer to 180°C/350°F. Line a deep non-stick 18cm (7in) baking tin (pan) with baking parchment and spray the sides lightly with oil.

2   Beat the eggs and cream in a bowl until they are well combined. Season with salt and pepper and stir in the cheese, ham, mushrooms, tomatoes, spring onions and herbs, distributing them throughout the mixture.

3   Transfer the mixture to the lined baking tin and lower it into the air fryer basket.

4   Cook the frittata in the air fryer for 12 minutes before checking whether it is ready (see tip). It should be set and golden brown on top. If not, cook it for another 2-4 minutes, checking it often.

5   Remove the frittata from the air fryer and set it aside to cool for 5 minutes before cutting it into wedges. Serve hot, warm or cold.

⭐ Tip: You can test whether the frittata is cooked by inserting a thin skewer or toothpick into the centre – it should come out clean.

VARIATIONS
• For a lighter, less creamy frittata, use milk instead of cream.
• Vary the flavours: try crumbled feta, diced red (bell) peppers or chillies, baby spinach or rocket leaves, and frozen peas.
• Add leftover cooked turkey, chicken or bacon.

CREAMY SCRAMBLED EGGS WITH SALMON AND AVOCADO

Scrambled eggs are light and fluffy when cooked in an air fryer. Try them yourself and see how delicious they are.

SERVES 2-3 / PREP: 10 MINUTES / COOK: 6-8 MINUTES

1 tbsp unsalted butter
4 medium free-range eggs
3 tbsp double (heavy) cream
    or milk
8 thin slices of smoked
    salmon
1 large ripe avocado, peeled,
    stoned (pitted) and sliced
sea salt and freshly ground
    black pepper

1   Heat the air fryer to 160°C/325°F. Put the butter into a non-stick baking tin (pan) and place it in the air fryer for 1–2 minutes, or until it melts. Brush the sides of the tin with the melted butter.

2   Whisk the eggs with the cream or milk in a jug. Season with salt and pepper.

3   Pour the mixture into the tin brushed with the melted butter and cook it for 2 minutes. Remove the tin from the air fryer and stir the mixture with a plastic or silicone spatula, scraping it off the sides and bottom.

4   Return it to the the air fryer and cook it for 2 more minutes, then stir again. Depending on how soft or well done you like your scrambled eggs, cook them for another 2–4 minutes, or longer, until they are the consistency you prefer.

5   Serve the eggs immediately with the smoked salmon and sliced avocado.

Tip: Remember to stir the eggs at 2-minute intervals to scramble them and prevent them sticking to the tin. Do not use a metal spoon as it will scratch the non-stick tin.

VARIATIONS
• Add some grated cheese or snipped chives, parsley or coriander (cilantro).
• Serve with crispy bacon or pancetta.

NO-PASTRY MINI BREAKFAST QUICHES

Eat these healthy crustless quiches hot or cold for breakfast – they keep well and can be made ahead of time and stored in the fridge overnight. Depending on the size of your air fryer, you may need to cook the quiches in two batches.

SERVES 4 / PREP: 10 MINUTES / COOK: 9-10 MINUTES

spray oil
2 medium free-range eggs
3 tbsp milk
1 spring onion (scallion), sliced
4 baby plum tomatoes, diced
50g (2oz) feta, crumbled
100g (3½oz) washed spinach
    leaves
a few sprigs of dill or basil,
    chopped
hot chilli sauce, for drizzling
    (optional)
freshly ground black pepper

1 Heat the air fryer to 180°C/350°F. Lightly spray 4 small non-stick muffin tins (pans) or ramekin dishes with oil.

2 Whisk the eggs and milk in a jug and stir in the spring onion, tomatoes and feta. Season with black pepper.

3 Put the spinach into a colander and pour some boiling water over the top until it wilts. Press down on the spinach with a saucer to squeeze out any excess moisture and then transfer it to a chopping board and chop it roughly. Stir it into the egg mixture with the chopped herbs.

4 Divide the mixture between the muffin tins or ramekin dishes and cook in the air fryer for 5 minutes. Remove the quiches from the air fryer and stir them gently, then cook them for 4-5 more minutes, or until they are set and golden brown on top.

5 Turn out the quiches and serve them immediately, drizzled with hot chilli sauce (if using). If you cooked the quiches in ramekins, you may prefer to eat them out of the dishes.

★ Tip: Feta is quite salty so don't add salt to the filling.

BREAKFAST BLT

This breakfast toastie can be enjoyed at any time of the day. And if you don't have bacon, use cooked sliced sausages instead, or try one of the vegetarian sandwich options below.

SERVES 4 / PREP: 10 MINUTES / COOK: 6-7 MINUTES

8 slices of streaky or back
    bacon
8 slices of wholegrain or
    multiseed bread
4 tbsp mayonnaise
a few crisp cos (romaine)
    or little gem lettuce leaves,
    shredded
2 ripe tomatoes, thinly sliced
1 small ripe avocado, peeled,
    stoned (pitted) and
    mashed
sea salt and freshly ground
    black pepper

1   Heat the air fryer to 190°C/375°F.

2   Place the bacon rashers in the air fryer in a single layer, leaving space around each rasher, and cook them for 3 minutes. Turn over the rashers and cook them for 3-4 minutes until they are crisp and golden brown. You may have to do this in two batches depending on the size of the basket.

3   Meanwhile, lightly toast the bread and spread 4 slices with the mayonnaise. Cover this with the lettuce and sliced tomatoes and season with salt and pepper. Top with the crispy bacon.

4   Spread the remaining pieces of toast with the mashed avocado and place them on top of the bacon.

5   Cut each sandwich in half or into quarters and serve immediately.

★ Tip: Vegetarians can substitute air-fried tofu or sliced boiled egg for the bacon.

VARIATIONS
• If you don't like avocado, use butter instead.
• Make it spicy by drizzling some sriracha or hot sauce over the bacon.
• Add some air-fried or roasted vegetables, e.g. peppers, aubergine (eggplant) or courgettes (zucchini).

TOFU SCRAMBLE

If you've never eaten scrambled tofu, now's the time to try it. It's so easy and a tasty vegan alternative to scrambled eggs, packed with protein and nutritional goodness. Serve it with air-fried vegetables or use it as a stuffing for wraps and pitta pockets.

SERVES 4 / PREP: 10 MINUTES / COOK: 10 MINUTES

4 tsp olive oil
1 tsp soy sauce or tamari
1 tsp ground turmeric
½ tsp ground cumin
½ tsp smoked paprika
a good pinch of garlic powder
1 tbsp nutritional yeast
400g (14oz) extra-firm or
    firm tofu
a few sprigs of parsley,
    chopped
sea salt and freshly ground
    black pepper

TO SERVE
air-fried tomatoes or
    mushrooms (see page 32)
    hash browns (see page 36)
hot sauce, for drizzling
    (optional)

1   Heat the air fryer to 190°C/375°F.

2   Put the oil, soy sauce or tamari, ground spices, garlic powder and nutritional yeast in a bowl. Add a little salt and pepper and stir well.

3   Crumble the tofu into the bowl with your hands and stir it gently until the pieces are evenly coated with the spice mixture.

4   Transfer the mixture to the air fryer (using a crisping tray if you have one) and cook it for 5 minutes. Remove the basket and stir the mixture well, shaking it a little. Replace it in the air fryer and cook it for 5 more minutes until it is golden and crispy.

5   Serve the tofu scramble sprinkled with parsley, with some air-fried cherry tomatoes or mushrooms and hash browns. Drizzle with hot sauce (if using).

★ Tip: Press the tofu block between sheets of kitchen paper (paper towels) to squeeze out any excess moisture.

VARIATIONS
• Add crushed chilli flakes to the spice mixture.
• Sprinkle with coriander (cilantro) or snipped chives.
• Serve with sliced avocado.

FULL ENGLISH BREAKFAST

You can make a full English breakfast in your air fryer with minimal oil. It's much lighter and healthier than the traditional fried one and even more delicious. Try it and see for yourself how good it is.

SERVES 2 / PREP: 10 MINUTES / COOK: 16-18 MINUTES

6 button mushrooms
spray oil
a handful of parsley, finely
    chopped
2 tomatoes, halved
2 pork sausages
4 slices of bacon
2 medium free-range eggs
sea salt and freshly ground
    black pepper

TO SERVE
buttered toast
tomato ketchup, mustard,
    Worcestershire sauce

1 Heat the air fryer to 180°C/350°F.

2 Place the button mushrooms on some kitchen foil and spray them lightly with oil. Season with salt and pepper, add the chopped parsley and fold the foil over the mushrooms to make a parcel, scrunching the edges.

3 Place the foil parcel, tomatoes and sausages in the air fryer and cook them for 5 minutes. Add the bacon and cook for 5 more minutes.

4 Spray 2 small ramekins lightly with oil. Measure 3 tablespoons of hot water into each ramekin and then crack an egg into each one.

5 Push the foil parcels, sausages and bacon to the side and place the ramekins in the basket. Cook for 6-8 minutes.

6 Divide the mushrooms, tomatoes, bacon and sausages between 2 serving plates. Use a small rubber spatula to ease the poached eggs out of the ramekins and place one on each plate. Serve immediately with buttered toast and the condiments of your choice.

VARIATIONS
• Sprinkle the mushrooms with crushed garlic and/or chopped herbs.

• Instead of poached eggs, place whole eggs in their shells in the basket at step 5 (above) and cook them for 6 minutes. To serve, place them in egg cups and slice off the tops.

STUFFED PORTOBELLO MUSHROOMS

You can serve these mushrooms with eggs and bacon for breakfast or enjoy them on toast as a snack at any time of day – either way, they're delicious. This recipe makes two portions eaten on its own, or serves four as part of a larger meal.

SERVES 2-4 / PREP: 10 MINUTES / COOK: 8-10 MINUTES

150g (5oz) spinach leaves, washed and trimmed
4 Portobello or large field mushrooms
2 garlic cloves, crushed
40g (1½oz/3 tbsp) butter, softened
2 tbsp crème fraîche
4 tbsp grated Cheddar cheese
spray oil
sea salt and freshly ground black pepper

1   Heat the air fryer to 180°C/350°F.

2   Put the spinach in a colander and pour boiling water over it until the leaves wilt. Press down firmly on the leaves with a saucer to extract all the moisture. Transfer the spinach to a chopping board and chop it coarsely.

3   Wipe the mushrooms clean and remove the stalks. Mash the garlic into the butter and stir in the crème fraîche and chopped spinach. Season with salt and pepper and then fill the mushroom caps with the mixture. Sprinkle the cheese over the top.

4   Lightly spray the air fryer basket with oil. Place the mushrooms in the basket – you may need to cook them in batches if you have a small basket. Cook them for 8–10 minutes, or until they are tender and golden on top. Serve with buttered toast.

★ Tip: Don't throw away the mushroom stalks. You can use them in soup or a pasta sauce.

VARIATIONS
• Use frozen spinach instead of fresh.
• Add some chopped herbs or diced bacon.
• Use diced mozzarella cheese or grated Parmesan.
• Substitute Greek yoghurt for the crème fraîche.

HASH BROWNS

Hash browns are quick and easy to make and taste so much better than supermarket frozen ones. They are the perfect accompaniment to eggs and bacon, or some smoked salmon with yoghurt or soured cream.

SERVES 4 / PREP: 10 MINUTES / SOAK: 10-15 MINUTES / COOK: 12-15 MINUTES

3 large Maris Piper, King Edward or Russet potatoes, peeled and coarsely grated (shredded)
1 tbsp plain (all-purpose) flour
1 medium free-range egg, beaten
spray oil
sea salt and freshly ground black pepper

1 Put the grated potato into a bowl and cover it with cold water. Stir, then set aside to soak for 10-15 minutes. Drain the potatoes and discard the soaking water.

2 Use a clean tea towel or kitchen paper (paper towels) to squeeze or press the moisture out of the grated potato a little at a time. When it's dry, place it in a clean bowl and stir in the flour and beaten egg. Season with salt and pepper

3 Divide the potato into 4 portions and shape them into patties with your hands.

4 Heat the air fryer to 200°C/400°F and lightly spray the basket with oil.

5 Place the patties in the basket, leaving a little space around each one. Spray them lightly with oil and cook them for 6 minutes. Take out the basket and flip the patties, then cook them for 6-9 minutes more, until they are crisp and golden brown all over.

★ Tip: Make sure you squeeze as much moisture as possible from the grated potatoes. This removes the starch and makes the hash browns crispy.

VARIATIONS
• Add some grated onion or garlic to the mixture before moulding it into patties.
• Stir a good pinch of cayenne or chilli powder into the mixture.

BREAKFAST BURRITOS

You can adapt these versatile burritos to include any food available, such as the leftovers from last night's dinner. Or you can serve them for lunch or dinner with a crisp salad or some colourful vegetables roasted in the air fryer.

SERVES 4 / PREP: 10 MINUTES / COOK: 11-15 MINUTES

1 tbsp unsalted butter
4 medium free-range eggs
3 tbsp double (heavy) cream
   or milk
a few sprigs of coriander
   (cilantro), chopped
2 spring onions (scallions),
   sliced
1 red chilli, deseeded and diced
4 tortillas
4 tbsp guacamole or smashed
   avocado (see page 24)
4 tbsp tomato salsa (pico de
   gallo)
50g (2oz/½ cup) grated
   Cheddar cheese
spray oil
sea salt and freshly ground
   black pepper

1 Heat the air fryer to 150°C/300°F. Put the butter in a non-stick baking tin (pan) and place it in the air fryer for 1–2 minutes, or until the butter melts. Brush the sides of the tin with the melted butter.

2 Whisk the eggs with the cream or milk in a jug. Mix in the coriander, spring onions and chilli, and season with salt and pepper.

3 Pour the mixture into the tin coated with the melted butter and cook it for 3 minutes. Remove the tin and stir the mixture with a plastic or silicone spatula, scraping the sides and bottom.

4 Cook for a further 3 minutes, then stir the mixture again. You may need to cook the eggs for another 3-6 minutes until they are the consistency you want.

5 Spread the tortillas with the guacamole or smashed avocado and drizzle them with the salsa. Top them with the scrambled eggs and cheese and then fold them over to enclose the filling. Lightly spray them with oil and place them in the air fryer basket.

6 Turn up the air fryer to 200°C/400°F and cook the burritos for 2–3 minutes until they are golden and crisp. Serve immediately.

VARIATIONS
- Drizzle the cooked burritos with hot sauce.
- Serve with soured cream or yoghurt.
- Add refried beans or black beans to the filling.

GRANOLA

This crunchy granola is so delicious and easy to make and, depending on the size of your air fryer, you could double the quantity as it keeps well in an airtight jar for up to two weeks.

SERVES 4 / PREP: 5 MINUTES / COOK: 9-11 MINUTES

100g (4oz/1¼ cups) rolled oats
50g (2oz/½ cup) chopped
    nuts, e.g. almonds, walnuts,
    hazelnuts or pecans
1 tsp ground cinnamon
a pinch of sea salt
3 tbsp maple syrup
2 tbsp coconut oil, melted
1 tsp vanilla extract
40g (1½oz/¼ cup) dried
    cranberries or raisins

TO SERVE
Greek yoghurt
blueberries, strawberries or
    raspberries

1   Heat the air fryer to 170°C/325°F.

2   Put the oats, nuts, cinnamon and sea salt in a bowl and stir well.

3   Mix together the maple syrup, coconut oil and vanilla extract and add to the dry ingredients. Mix well until everything is lightly coated.

4   Line the air fryer basket with baking parchment and spoon the granola mixture into the basket, spreading it out in an even layer.

5   Cook the mixture for 5 minutes and then take out the basket and shake it well. Cook it for 4–6 minutes more, until the mixture is crisp and golden.

6   Leave the granola to cool in the basket and then stir in the dried fruit. Store it in an airtight jar or container.

★ Tip: Keep checking the granola as it cooks and shake the basket frequently to prevent it over-browning or burning.

VARIATIONS
• Use a light olive oil or avocado oil instead of coconut oil.

• Add some peanut or almond butter to the mixture.

• Stir in some pumpkin pie spice.

• Mix some dark chocolate chips or mixed seeds into the cooked granola.

• Substitute honey for the maple syrup (though it won't be vegan).

LIGHT MEALS

You won't need to give up your favourite quick and easy meals if you follow these recipes! There are tips on how to avoid ultra-processed ingredients while still enjoying food such as hot dogs or chicken nuggets. You can forget about food containing high levels of sodium, fats or nitrates. An air fryer does an amazing job and these recipes will replicate your store-bought favourites so well that you won't be able to taste the difference!

BEEFBURGERS

Use the best-quality minced (ground) beef you can find to make really tasty burgers – beef chuck is best of all. For juicy burgers, look for mince with 20 per cent fat. Cooking them in an air fryer makes them deliciously crisp on the outside while keeping them juicy and succulent inside.

SERVES 4 / PREP: 10 MINUTES / COOK: 7-9 MINUTES

500g (1lb 2oz/generous 2 cups) minced (ground) beef
1 small free-range egg, beaten
spray oil
4 burger buns
4 tbsp mustard mayo, e.g. Dijonnaise
4 crisp lettuce leaves
1 tomato, thickly sliced
thinly sliced red onion (optional)
sliced gherkins or dill pickles (optional)
tomato ketchup, for drizzling
sea salt and freshly ground black pepper

1　Mix the minced beef with enough of the beaten egg to bind it together and then season it generously with salt and pepper.

2　Divide the mixture into 4 equal portions and shape them into round patties with your hands. Spray them lightly with oil.

3　Heat the air fryer to 200°C/400°F.

4　Place the burgers in the air fryer basket in a single layer with space between them and cook for 4 minutes. Flip them over and cook them for a further 3–5 minutes, depending on how well you like them cooked.

5　Split the burger buns (and toast them if you like them toasted) then spread each base with the mustard mayo. Place a lettuce leaf on top and then a slice of tomato and some sliced red onion, gherkins or dill pickles (if using). Place a burger on top and cover it with the top of the bun. Serve immediately with ketchup on the side.

VARIATIONS
• To make cheeseburgers, place a slice of cheese on top of each burger for the final 5 minutes of cooking in the air fryer.

• Top the burgers with garlic butter or drizzle them with BBQ or hot sauce.

• Add some ranch or thousand island dressing.

• Add some crispy bacon rashers, fried onions or mushrooms.

• Add some mashed avocado, guacamole or coleslaw.

CHICKEN NUGGETS WITH HONEY MUSTARD DIP

Who doesn't like chicken nuggets? These are super delicious and healthier than many supermarket and takeaway nuggets, which are sometimes made with ultra-processed meat. Enjoy them as a light meal with salad and fries cooked in the air fryer or as finger food with this easy honey mustard dip.

SERVES 4 / PREP: 20 MINUTES / COOK: 8-12 MINUTES

50g (2oz/½ cup) plain (all-purpose) flour
1 tsp smoked paprika
2 medium free-range eggs
200g (7oz/2 cups) panko breadcrumbs
500g (1lb 2oz) skinless chicken breasts, cut into 4cm (1½in) cubes
spray oil
sea salt and freshly ground black pepper

HONEY MUSTARD DIP
240ml (8fl oz/1 cup) mayonnaise
2 tbsp honey mustard
freshly ground black pepper

1   Mix the mayonnaise with the honey mustard in a bowl. Season to taste with black pepper, and add more mayo or mustard until the dip has the right consistency and flavour. Cover it and chill it in the fridge until you are ready to eat.

2   Sift the flour into a bowl and stir in the smoked paprika. Beat the eggs in a separate bowl. Mix the panko breadcrumbs with the salt and pepper in another bowl.

3   Dust the chicken cubes with flour, shaking off any excess, and dip them in the beaten egg and then the breadcrumbs until they are coated all over. Spray them lightly with oil.

4   Heat the air fryer to 200°C/400°F.

5   Place the chicken nuggets in the air fryer basket in a single layer with a little space between them – you may have to cook them in batches depending on the size of your air fryer. Cook the nuggets for about 4 minutes and then turn them over. Cook them for another 4–8 minutes until they are cooked through and crisp and golden.

6   Serve the nuggets hot with the honey mustard dip, or tomato ketchup if you prefer.

BEEF KOFTAS WITH RAITA

Spicy koftas are easy to make and cook fast in an air fryer. You can make them in advance and store them in a sealed container in the fridge until you're ready to cook them later in the day.

SERVES 4 / PREP: 15 MINUTES / COOK: 9-10 MINUTES

500g (1lb 2oz/generous 2 cups) minced (ground) beef
1 small red onion, grated
2 garlic cloves, crushed
1 chilli, diced
1 tsp ground cumin
1 tsp ground coriander
a handful of coriander (cilantro), chopped
spray oil
sea salt and freshly ground black pepper
boiled rice or salad, to serve

CUCUMBER RAITA

200g (7oz/scant 1 cup) 0% fat Greek yoghurt
a handful of mint, chopped
¼ cucumber, diced
1 garlic clove, crushed
3 spring onions (scallions), sliced
a pinch of ground cumin

1 Make the raita: mix all the ingredients in a bowl, adding salt to taste. Chill it in the fridge until you're ready to eat.

2 Heat the air fryer to 180°C/350°F.

3 Put the minced beef, onion, garlic, chilli, ground spices and chopped coriander in a bowl. Mix well and season with salt and pepper. Use your hands to mould the mixture into 4 sausage shapes. Thread them on to metal skewers and spray them lightly with oil. Alternatively, you can mould the mixture into 8 smaller sausage shapes and thread 2 on to each skewer.

4 Place the koftas in the air fryer, with a little space between them – you may have to cook them in batches depending on the size of your air fryer. Cook them for 5 minutes. Flip them over and cook them for a further 4–5 minutes until they are browned and cooked to your liking.

5 Serve with the raita and some boiled rice or salad.

⭐ Tip: Chill the koftas in the fridge for 30 minutes to firm them before cooking.

VARIATIONS
• Serve with lime pickle or mango chutney.
• Add some ground turmeric to the beef mixture.
• Serve them Greek style with tzatziki and add some dried oregano and mint to the beef mixture.
• Substitute minced lamb for the beef.

CHICKEN SHAWARMA WRAPS

Spicy, aromatic shawarma chicken is popular throughout the Middle East. It's so delicious and easy to make. Use chicken thighs in preference to breast meat as they are more flavoursome, juicy and succulent.

SERVES 4 / PREP: 10 MINUTES / MARINATE: 30 MINUTES / COOK: 20-22 MINUTES

500g (1lb 2oz) skinless, boneless chicken thighs
4 large wraps, warmed
8 tbsp hummus
shredded lettuce
thinly sliced red onion
Greek yoghurt and hot sauce, for drizzling

SPICY MARINADE
1 tsp sumac
1 tsp sweet paprika
½ tsp ras el hanout
½ tsp ground turmeric
½ tsp ground cumin
a pinch of ground cinnamon
juice of 1 large lemon
2 tbsp olive oil
4 garlic cloves, crushed
sea salt and freshly ground black pepper

1 Make the marinade: mix the spices with the lemon juice, olive oil and garlic. Season with salt and pepper.

2 Add the chicken pieces and stir until they are well coated with the marinade. Leave them to stand at room temperature for at least 30 minutes.

3 Heat the air fryer to 200°C/400°F.

4 Place the marinated chicken pieces in the air fryer in a single layer – you may have to cook them in batches depending on the size of your air fryer. Cook them for 10 minutes, then flip them over and cook them for a further 10–12 minutes until they are cooked through and golden brown.

5 Set the chicken pieces aside to rest for 10 minutes and then cut them into thin slices.

6 Spread the hummus over the warm wraps and top them with the chicken slices, lettuce and red onion. Drizzle them with yoghurt and hot sauce, then roll them up or fold them over. Serve immediately.

★ Tip: You can cover the marinated chicken and chill it in the fridge overnight.

VARIATIONS
• Serve with fiery harissa instead of hot sauce.
• Use tahini drizzle (see page 136) instead of yoghurt.
• Add some roasted aubergine (eggplant), sliced (bell) peppers or courgettes (zucchini).

LAMB PITTA POCKETS

Stuffed pittas are perfect for a delicious light meal or food to eat on the go when you're out and about. You could cook the lamb balls in advance and then assemble the pittas to enjoy as a packed lunch the following day.

SERVES 4 / PREP: 20 MINUTES / CHILL: 15 MINUTES / COOK: 9-10 MINUTES

500g (1lb 2oz/generous 2 cups) minced (ground) lamb
1 small onion, grated
1 tsp ground cumin
½ tsp cayenne
a pinch of fennel seeds
a few sprigs of mint, chopped
a few sprigs of flat-leaf parsley, chopped
grated zest of 1 lemon
spray oil
4 wholemeal pitta breads
crisp salad leaves, e.g. cos (romaine) or little gem lettuce
sea salt and freshly ground black pepper

TZATZIKI

200g (7oz/scant 1 cup) 0% fat Greek yoghurt
1 tbsp olive oil
½ cucumber, diced
2 garlic cloves, crushed
a handful of dill, chopped
juice of ½ lemon

1. Make the tzatziki: mix all the ingredients in a bowl, adding salt to taste. Chill the tzatziki in the fridge until you're ready to eat.

2. Mix the lamb, onion, spices, herbs, lemon zest and seasoning in a bowl. Divide the mixture into 8 equal portions and mould them into balls with your hands. Chill them in the fridge for 15 minutes to firm up.

3. Heat the air fryer to 190°C/375°F.

4. Spray the balls lightly with oil and place them in the air fryer, with a little space between them. You may have to cook them in batches depending on the size of your air fryer. Cook them for 5 minutes, then flip them over and cook them for a further 4–5 minutes until they are brown and cooked through.

5. Warm and split the pitta breads and fill them with the hot lamb balls, salad leaves and tzatziki.

VARIATIONS
• Serve with tahini drizzle (see page 136).
• Use wraps or tortillas instead of pittas.
• Add some tomatoes and avocado to the pitta filling.
• Substitute hummus for tzatziki.

HOT DOGS

Use good-quality premium pork sausages with natural skins and no additives to make these hot dogs. They are healthy, delicious and nutritious – better than frankfurters, which are highly processed and often contain high levels of sodium, fat and nitrates.

SERVES 4 / PREP: 5 MINUTES / COOK: 20-24 MINUTES

1 large onion, thinly sliced
2 tsp olive oil, plus extra for
    spraying
4 fat pork sausages
4 mini baguettes (French
    sticks)
sea salt and freshly ground
    black pepper
tomato ketchup, for drizzling
mustard, for drizzling

1   Heat the air fryer to 190°C/375°F.

2   Put the onion slices, olive oil and salt and pepper in a bowl. Toss them well until the onions are coated with oil.

3   Place the onions in the air fryer basket and cook them for 10–12 minutes. Shake them every 3–4 minutes, and spray them lightly with oil halfway through. When they are golden and slightly crispy, remove them from the air fryer and keep warm while you cook the sausages.

4   Heat the air fryer to 200°C/400°F.

5   Place the sausages in the basket with a little space between them. Cook them for 10–12 minutes, shaking them a few times, until they are evenly browned all over and cooked through.

6   Split open the baguettes and cover the bases with the fried onions. Place a sausage on top of each one and drizzle it with ketchup and mustard. Cover them with the top halves of the baguettes. No need for knives and forks – this is perfect finger food.

> **VARIATIONS**
> • Stir a few drops of syrupy balsamic vinegar into the fried onions.
> • Drizzle with hot sauce, BBQ sauce or spicy tomato relish.
> • Instead of onions, add some coleslaw or sauerkraut.
> • Use soft hot dog buns instead of crisp baguettes.

TOFU SKEWERS WITH SATAY SAUCE

This is a great veggie dish for when you're in a hurry. You can make the satay sauce in advance but the tofu should be eaten freshly cooked and really hot to enjoy it at its crispy best. Alternatively, serve the skewers drizzled with sweet chilli sauce or sriracha.

SERVES 4 / PREP: 15 MINUTES / COOK: 10-12 MINUTES

400g (14oz) extra-firm tofu, pressed (see tip)
1 tsp light soy sauce
1 tbsp cornflour (cornstarch)
1 tsp smoked paprika
½ tsp garlic powder
½ tsp sesame oil
sea salt flakes and freshly ground black pepper
chopped coriander (cilantro), to garnish
noodles or rice, to serve

QUICK SATAY SAUCE
150g (5oz/generous ½ cup) crunchy peanut butter
50g (2oz) creamed coconut, grated
2 garlic cloves, crushed
juice of 1 lime
2 tbsp dark soy sauce
2 tbsp sweet chilli sauce
1-2 tbsp cold water

1   Make the satay sauce: whisk together the peanut butter, coconut, garlic, lime juice, soy sauce and sweet chilli sauce. Thin the sauce to a dipping consistency with cold water and then set it aside.

2   Pat the tofu dry with kitchen paper (paper towels) and cut it into 2cm (¾in) cubes. Place the cubes in a bowl and toss them gently in the soy sauce, then add the cornflour, smoked paprika, garlic powder and oil. Toss the cubes until they are lightly coated all over. Thread them on to 8 skewers that fit inside the air fryer, leaving a small space between each tofu cube – don't thread them too tightly.

3   Heat the air fryer to 190°C/375°F.

4   Place the skewers in the air fryer in a single layer – you may have to cook them in batches depending on the size of your air fryer. Cook them for 5 minutes and then flip them over and cook them for 5-7 minutes more until they are crisp and golden brown.

5   Season with sea salt flakes and some black pepper and scatter over the coriander. Serve immediately with the satay sauce and some noodles or rice.

★ Tip: Block tofu is usually packed in water, so you need to press it before using. Drain and cut the block into 4 slices, then place in a single layer between 2 sheets of kitchen paper (paper towel). Cover with a clean cloth and weight this down with books or tins. Leave for 30 minutes, drain the water and it's ready to use.

THAI CRAB CAKES WITH DIPPING SAUCE

These aromatic crab cakes are a quick and easy lunch – or you can make them smaller and serve them as an appetizer or with pre-dinner drinks. They are lower in fat than fried crab cakes, so they are healthier but retain their crispness. If you can't find fresh crab meat, you can use tinned or frozen instead. Use a mixture of white and brown meat.

SERVES 4 / PREP: 15 MINUTES / COOK: 10-12 MINUTES

450g (1lb) fresh crab meat
1 red chilli, deseeded and
    roughly chopped
3 spring onions (scallions),
    chopped
2 garlic cloves, crushed
a handful of coriander
    (cilantro)
1 tbsp nam pla (Thai fish
    sauce)
50g (2oz/¼ cup) mayonnaise
50g (2oz/½ cup) panko
    breadcrumbs
3-4 tbsp flour
spray oil

DIPPING SAUCE
2 tbsp rice vinegar
1 tsp sugar
1 tsp dark soy sauce
1 red chilli, diced
juice of 1 lime

1   Make the dipping sauce: heat the rice vinegar and sugar in a small saucepan, stirring until the sugar dissolves. When the mixture becomes syrupy, stir in the soy sauce, chilli and lime juice. Remove the pan from the heat and set it aside to cool.

2   Put the crab meat, chilli, spring onions, garlic, coriander, nam pla and mayonnaise in a food processor and pulse to a thick sludge. Transfer the mixture to a bowl and stir in the breadcrumbs and flour. If the mixture is too dry, add more mayonnaise; if it's too wet, add more flour.

3   Divide the mixture into 8 equal portions and shape them into patties with your hands. Spray them lightly with oil.

4   Heat the air fryer to 180°C/350°F.

5   Place the crab cakes in a single layer in the air fryer basket with a little space between them – you may have to cook them in batches depending on the size of your air fryer. Cook the cakes for about 5 minutes and then turn them over. Cook them for another 5–7 minutes until they are crisp and golden brown.

6   Serve the crab cakes immediately with the dipping sauce. Boiled rice and a crisp Thai salad make good accompaniments.

VARIATIONS
• Serve with stir-fried greens or air-fried broccoli.
• Serve with sweet chilli dipping sauce.

BUTTERNUT SQUASH SOUP

It's easy to make vegetable soup in an air fryer with minimal effort and fuss. Just roast the vegetables, then blitz them with stock in a food processor before warming the soup through and adding some spices. Hey presto! It's ready.

SERVES 4-6 /PREP: 15 MINUTES / COOK: 20-30 MINUTES

1 onion, thickly sliced
2 carrots, thickly sliced
1kg (2lb 4oz) butternut squash, peeled, deseeded and cubed
2 garlic cloves, peeled
a pinch of dried thyme
2 tbsp olive oil
750ml (1¼ pints/generous 3 cups) hot vegetable stock
2 tsp ground turmeric
1 tsp ground cumin
½ tsp grated nutmeg
¼ tsp ground cinnamon
120ml (4fl oz/½ cup) milk
sea salt and freshly ground black pepper
crisp croutons, to serve (optional)
pumpkin seeds, to serve (optional)
crème fraîche, to serve (optional)

1 Put the prepared vegetables, garlic and thyme in a bowl and toss them in the olive oil. Season with a little salt and pepper.

2 Heat the air fryer to 200°C/400°F.

3 Put the vegetables in the air fryer basket and cook them for 20-30 minutes, taking out the basket and shaking it several times, until the vegetables are cooked and tender.

4 Transfer the mixture to a food processor and pulse until it's smooth, gradually adding the vegetable stock.

5 Pour the soup into a saucepan set over a low to medium heat and stir in the ground spices and milk. Heat it through gently and let it simmer for 5 minutes so the flavours mingle. Check the seasoning, adding more salt and pepper if needed.

6 Ladle the soup into bowls and serve topped with the croutons, pumpkin seeds and crème fraîche (if using).

VARIATIONS
• Use coconut milk instead of dairy or plant milk.
• Add ground ginger or sweet paprika.
• Top with air-fried mushrooms, pumpkin seeds or crumbled crispy bacon.
• Add cubed sweet potato.

MELANZANE PARMIGIANA

To make this traditional southern Italian recipe you will need a baking dish that fits inside your air fryer. It's the perfect food for al fresco summer lunches and buffets, served with a salad – or it's also delicious on chilly winter evenings. Even people who usually don't like aubergines (eggplants) usually enjoy it.

SERVES 4 / PREP: 15 MINUTES / COOK: 12-18 MINUTES

2 large aubergines (eggplants)
olive oil spray
a few fresh basil leaves
300g (10oz) fresh mozzarella,
    sliced
2-3 tbsp grated Parmesan
sea salt and freshly ground
    black pepper

TOMATO SAUCE
300g (10oz/1¼ cups) tinned
    chopped tomatoes, strained
a squeeze of garlic purée
a pinch of sugar
1 tsp dried oregano or marjoram
1 tbsp olive oil

VARIATIONS
• Add some Italian seasoning to the tomato sauce.

• Sprinkle some fresh white breadcrumbs over the top and spray them with oil.

• Use grated pecorino or Grana Padano instead of Parmesan.

1 Make the tomato sauce: mix all the ingredients in a bowl and season the sauce with salt and pepper.

2 Cut the aubergine into 5mm (¼in) thick slices. Spray them with olive oil on both sides and sprinkle them with sea salt.

3 Heat the air fryer to 200°C/400°F.

4 Lightly spray the air fryer basket with oil. Place the aubergine slices in the basket in a single layer with a little space between them – you may have to cook them in batches depending on the size of your air fryer. Cook them for 3-4 minutes, then flip them over and cook them for a further 2-3 minutes until they are lightly browned.

5 Cover the base of a baking dish that fits inside your air fryer with half the aubergine slices. Pour the tomato sauce over the top and cover it with the basil leaves and most of the mozzarella. Place the remaining aubergine slices and mozzarella on top and sprinkle them with Parmesan.

6 Cook the parmigiana in the air fryer for 6-8 minutes until it's golden brown and crisp on top. Serve immediately.

★ Tip: You can scale down the recipe for small air fryers.

TURKEY BURGERS

These burgers are 100 per cent pure turkey meat and flavoured with onions and herbs. They are super healthy and easy to make – perfect for brunch or a light family supper served with a crisp salad.

SERVES 4 / PREP: 10 MINUTES / CHILL: 20-30 MINUTES / COOK: 15-16 MINUTES

500g (1lb 2oz/generous 2 cups) minced (ground) turkey
2 spring onions (scallions), finely chopped
1 garlic clove, crushed
a handful of parsley, finely chopped
a handful of mint, finely chopped
spray oil
4 burger buns
sea salt and freshly ground black pepper

TOPPINGS
sliced Cheddar cheese, melted
crisp lettuce, sliced tomato and red onion
ketchup, sriracha mayo, mustard or tomato relish

1   Mix the minced turkey, spring onions, garlic and herbs in a bowl. Season with salt and pepper.

2   Divide the mixture into 4 equal portions and shape each one into a burger with your hands. Chill the burgers in the fridge for 20–30 minutes until they are firm.

3   Heat the air fryer to 190°C/375°F.

4   Spray the burgers lightly with oil and place them in the basket with a little space between them – you may have to cook them in batches depending on the size of your air fryer. Cook the burgers for 8 minutes, then flip them over and cook them for a further 7–8 minutes until they are golden brown and cooked through.

5   Split the buns and place a turkey burger in each one, plus the toppings of your choice. For cheeseburgers, top each cooked burger with a cheese slice and air fry for 1 minute.

⭐ Tip: The turkey must be finely minced or the burger may fall apart. If you can't buy ready-minced turkey blitz some skinned and boned turkey thighs or breast in a food processor.

VARIATIONS
• Use minced chicken instead of turkey.
• Add lemon zest or grated Parmesan to the burger mixture.
• Spice it up with some diced hot chilli.
• Use coriander (cilantro) and serve drizzled with Thai chilli sauce.

QUICK PIZZA POCKETS

Deliciously tasty pizza pockets are popular with adults and children alike. Serve them as a light lunch or supper dish with salad and vegetables, or as a snack or party food with a dipping sauce.

SERVES 4 / PREP: 20 MINUTES / COOK: 10-12 MINUTES

500g (1lb 2oz) pizza dough (see tip below or page 149)
100g (4oz) cooked ham, diced
100g (4oz/1 cup) grated (shredded) mozzarella
1 medium free-range egg, beaten
spray oil

PIZZA SAUCE
50g (2oz/¼ cup) tomato purée (paste)
75g (3oz/⅓ cup) tinned chopped tomatoes, strained
a pinch of sugar
a pinch of dried oregano
1 tbsp olive oil
sea salt and freshly ground black pepper

1 Make the pizza sauce: mix all the ingredients together in a bowl, adding salt and pepper to taste.

2 Lightly flour a clean work surface and roll out the pizza dough until it is 5mm (¼in) thick. Cut out 8 circles with a 10cm (4in) pastry cutter.

3 Spread the pizza sauce over each circle of dough, leaving a border around the edge. Sprinkle the bases with the cooked ham and top them with the mozzarella. Fold the dough over the filling to completely enclose it and pinch the edges together to seal them. Lightly brush the dough with beaten egg.

4 Heat the air fryer to 180°C/350°F.

5 Lightly spray the air fryer basket with oil. Place the pizza pockets in the basket in a single layer with a little space between them – you may have to cook them in batches depending on the size of your air fryer. Cook them for 8–10 minutes, then turn them over and cook them for 2 more minutes to brown the other side.

6 Serve immediately with a crisp salad.

⭐ Tip: You don't have to make the pizza dough yourself – most supermarkets sell fresh or frozen pizza dough.

MAIN MEALS

This chapter includes traditional recipes along with some for your favourite takeaways. Don't worry about cooking with too much oil or using additives – the recipes here will answer all your cravings. An air fryer cooks dishes much faster than a conventional oven and you don't have to compromise on taste. Fresh ingredients offer you much greater depth of flavour so there's no need for ready-made sauces and you can cut out ultra-processed food completely. Enjoy favourites such as fish and chips and peri peri chicken cooked at home – and made even more delicious by using authentic ingredients and your air fryer.

TERIYAKI CHICKEN SKEWERS

Homemade teriyaki sauce is better for you and tastier than shop-bought and it only takes a few minutes to make yourself. If you have some marinade left over brush it over the cooked chicken skewers before sprinkling them with sesame seeds.

SERVES 4 / PREP: 10 MINUTES / CHILL: 1 HOUR / COOK: 12-15 MINUTES

4 tbsp soy sauce
2 tbsp mirin
1 tbsp clear honey
1 tbsp light brown sugar
2 tsp grated fresh root ginger
2 garlic cloves, crushed
450g (1lb) skinless boneless
    chicken thighs, cut into
    2.5cm (1in) cubes
sesame seeds, for sprinkling

TO SERVE
boiled rice or rice noodles
mangetout or sugar snap peas
    (snow peas)
shredded deseeded red
    chillies and spring
    onions (scallions)

1 Mix the soy sauce, mirin, honey, sugar, ginger and garlic in a large bowl. Stir in the chicken pieces and make sure they are completely coated with the marinade. Cover the bowl and chill the chicken in the fridge for 1 hour.

2 Thread the chicken pieces on to 4 long or 8 small wooden, bamboo or metal skewers (see tip below).

3 Heat the air fryer to 190°C/375°F.

4 Place the chicken skewers in the basket in a single layer, leaving a little space between them – you may have to cook them in batches depending on the size of your air fryer. Cook them for 12–15 minutes, turning them after 6 minutes, until the chicken is cooked through.

5 Sprinkle the chicken pieces with sesame seeds and serve them immediately with rice or noodles and mangetout or sugar snap peas. Scatter some shredded chillies and spring onions over the top.

Tip: Soak wooden or bamboo skewers in a bowl of water for 30 minutes before using them to prevent them burning during cooking.

VARIATIONS
• Use turkey or steak instead of chicken.
• Chicken breasts also work well although they are not as juicy as thighs.

ROAST CHICKEN

A whole roast chicken is one of the most delicious and simple meals you can make. In less than an hour, an air fryer cooks chicken to perfection – with golden brown, crisp, crunchy skin and moist, tender meat underneath. This recipe flavours it with garlic butter, fresh herbs and lemon, but feel free to experiment with any rubs, herbs and spices you have to hand.

SERVES 4 / PREP: 10 MINUTES / COOK: 45-50 MINUTES / REST: 10 MINUTES

2 tbsp butter, softened
2 garlic cloves, crushed
1.5kg (3lb 5oz) free-range chicken, at room temperature
a few sprigs of thyme and rosemary
1 lemon, halved
avocado or olive oil spray
sea salt and freshly ground black pepper

1 Heat the air fryer to 190°C/375°F.

2 Mix the softened butter with the crushed garlic. Lift the chicken skin covering the breasts and slide the garlic butter underneath, so it sits between the skin and the flesh.

3 Place the herbs and lemon halves inside the cavity. Lightly spray the chicken with oil and grind sea salt and black pepper all over it.

4 Place the chicken in the air fryer basket, breast-side down, and cook it for 25 minutes. Turn it over and cook it breast up for a further 20–25 minutes, or until the skin is golden brown and crisp and the meat is cooked through but still moist.

5 Remove the chicken from the basket and set it aside to rest for 10 minutes before carving. Serve it with a green salad or vegetables and roast potatoes.

★ Tip: To check that the chicken is cooked, insert a meat thermometer into the thigh. If it hits 75°C/165°F, the chicken ready. Alternatively you can insert a thin sharp knife into the space between the thigh and the breast. If the juices run clear, the chicken is cooked.

VARIATIONS
• You can use a spice rub on the chicken before roasting, e.g. Italian seasoning or some garlic powder.
• Fill the cavity with sprigs of tarragon, oregano or marjoram.

TRADITIONAL ROAST SIRLOIN OF BEEF

If you love thinly sliced rare roast beef, follow this recipe and cook the joint in your air fryer. You want to choose a prime cut that does not need slow cooking, such as rolled sirloin, rib or topside. It will cook evenly and stay juicy inside while being deliciously crisp on the outside. Once you've tried it, you'll be a convert and will never use an oven again.

SERVES 6 / PREP: 5 MINUTES / COOK: 40-60 MINUTES, DEPENDING ON DONENESS (SEE BELOW) / REST: 15 MINUTES

1kg (2¼lb) rolled sirloin of beef
    joint, at room temperature
1 tsp dried oregano, rosemary
    or thyme
olive oil, for drizzling
sea salt and freshly ground
    black pepper
mustard or horseradish,
    to serve

1 Heat the air fryer to 200°C/400°F.

2 Dry the beef by patting the joint with kitchen paper (paper towels), then season it with dried herbs and plenty of salt and pepper, and finally drizzle it with oil, rubbing it in with your hands. Alternatively, put the seasoning and oil on a plate and roll the beef in it.

3 Put the beef in the air fryer basket and cook it for 10 minutes. Lower the temperature to 180°C/350°F and cook it for 30-35 minutes more for rare roast beef. If you prefer your beef medium rare add another 5 minutes; add an extra 10 minutes for medium or 15 minutes for well done beef.

4 Remove the beef from the air fryer, cover it with kitchen foil and set it aside to rest for 15 minutes before carving.

5 Serve it with a salad or with roast potatoes, Yorkshire puddings, vegetables and gravy, accompanied by mustard or horseradish.

★ Tip: You can test the beef with a meat thermometer to check for doneness. For rare roast beef, it should read 52-54°C/126-129°F.

VARIATIONS
• Add some garlic or onion powder to the seasoning mixture.
• Spice it up with smoked paprika, cayenne or ground cumin.

SEARED STEAK

Steaks cooked in an air fryer are juicy and tender inside and beautifully seared outside. Crisp air fryer chips or French fries and a healthy salad are a great accompaniment. Alternatively, slice the steaks tagliata-style and serve them with peppery rocket and sweet cherry tomatoes drizzled with balsamic vinegar.

SERVES 4 / PREP: 5 MINUTES / COOK: 4-12 MINUTES, DEPENDING ON DONENESS (SEE BELOW) / REST: 5-10 MINUTES

4 x 225g (8oz) sirloin or fillet steaks about 2.5cm (1in) thick, at room temperature
spray olive oil
sea salt and freshly ground black pepper

TO SERVE
French fries or chips (see pages 116–117)
mustard, béarnaise sauce or ketchup

1 Heat the air fryer to 200°C/400°F.

2 Pat the steaks dry with kitchen paper (paper towels) and spray both sides lightly with oil. Rub in the oil and season the steaks with plenty of salt and pepper.

3 Put the steaks in the air fryer in a single layer, leaving a little space between them – you may have to cook them in batches depending on the size of your air fryer. Cook rare steaks for 4–6 minutes; medium rare steaks for 6–8 minutes; medium steaks for 8–10 minutes; and well done steaks for 10–12 minutes.

4 Rest the steaks, covered with kitchen foil, for at least 5 minutes before serving them with French fries or chips and sauces or condiments.

★ Tip: Keep checking your steaks to make sure you don't overcook them. Air fryer models differ and some cook faster than others.

VARIATIONS
• Use a spicy rub or some steak seasoning.
• Top each steak with a pat of garlic and herb butter: mix softened butter with crushed garlic and finely chopped herbs, e.g. parsley, chives or tarragon.
• Garlic mushrooms or grilled cherry tomatoes make a good accompaniment.

BANGERS AND MASH WITH ONION GRAVY

Sausage and mash is the ultimate comfort food on a cold day. It's soothing, sustaining and simple to make, and crisp air fryer sausages are the best you will ever eat – they stay perfectly moist and juicy inside. Make sure you buy good-quality, well-seasoned sausages, preferably from the butcher and not the cheap ultra-processed sausages sold in some supermarkets.

SERVES 4 / PREP: 10 MINUTES / COOK: 20-25 MINUTES

900g (2lb) potatoes, e.g. Maris
    Piper or King Edward, peeled
    and cut into large chunks
75ml (3fl oz/generous ¼ cup) milk
15g (½oz/1 tbsp) butter
8 good-quality pork sausages
sea salt and freshly ground
    black pepper

ONION GRAVY
3 tbsp olive oil
2 large onions, thinly sliced
2 tbsp plain (all-purpose) flour
300ml (½ pint/1¼ cups) hot
    beef, chicken or vegetable
    stock
1–2 tbsp syrupy balsamic vinegar

VARIATIONS
• Use red onions instead of white in the gravy.

• Use red or white wine vinegar instead of balsamic vinegar, or sweeten the gravy with a spoonful of redcurrant jelly or cranberry sauce.

• Add some crushed garlic and crème fraîche to the mashed potatoes.

1 Half-fill a large saucepan with salted water and bring it to the boil. Add the potatoes and boil them for 12–15 minutes until they are tender. Drain them in a colander and then return them to the hot pan with the milk and butter. Off the heat, mash the potatoes with a potato masher and beat them with a wooden spoon or an electric whisk until they are smooth, creamy and lump-free. Season them to taste with salt and pepper and keep them warm.

2 While the potatoes are cooking make the gravy: heat the oil in a frying pan (skillet) set over a low heat. Add the onions and cook them for 15 minutes, stirring occasionally, until they are tender and starting to caramelize.

3 Stir in the flour and cook it for 1 minute. Gradually stir in the stock and vinegar and increase the heat to high. Bring the gravy to the boil, stirring, then reduce the heat and simmer it gently for 4–5 minutes until it is thickened and smooth. Season to taste with salt and pepper.

4 Towards the end of the cooking times for the potatoes and gravy, heat the air fryer to 200°C/400°F.

5 Put the sausages in the air fryer in a single layer, leaving a little space between them – you may have to cook them in batches depending on the size of your air fryer. Cook them for 10–12 minutes, turning them 2 or 3 times, until they are golden brown and cooked through.

6 Serve with the mashed potato and onion gravy and some green beans, Brussels sprouts or broccoli.

MEXICAN CHICKEN FAJITAS

Air fryer fajitas use less oil than pan-fried ones and are healthier. They're great to serve for TV suppers as they can be eaten by hand and everyone can help themselves to the filling and toppings and roll their own. Vegetarians can replace the chicken with tofu, or just sprinkle the vegetables with plenty of grated cheese.

SERVES 4 / PREP: 10 MINUTES / CHILL: 30 MINUTES / COOK: 15–18 MINUTES

500g (1lb 2oz) skinless chicken breast fillets, cut into thin strips
juice of 1 lime
1 tsp ground cumin
½ tsp smoked paprika
¼ tsp chilli powder
1 red onion, thinly sliced
1 green, red or yellow (bell) pepper, into strips
2 red (bell) peppers, deseeded and cut into strips
1 tbsp olive oil
sea salt and freshly ground black pepper

TO SERVE
warm tortillas
spicy salsa or pico de gallo
soured cream
guacamole
chilli flakes
coriander (cilantro) leaves

1 Put the chicken strips, lime juice and ground spices into a bowl. Stir, then cover and chill the bowl in the fridge for at least 30 minutes.

2 Stir in the onion, peppers and olive oil, and season with salt and pepper.

3 Heat the air fryer to 200°C/400°F.

4 Put the chicken and vegetables in the air fryer. Unless you have a very large basket, you will have to cook them in batches – do not overcrowd the basket or they will not cook evenly. Cook them for 15–18 minutes, tossing them occasionally, until the vegetables are tender and the chicken is golden brown and cooked through.

5 Warm the tortillas and divide the chicken and vegetable mixture between them. Top them with salsa or pico de gallo, soured cream, guacamole, chilli flakes and a few coriander leaves, and fold them over or roll them up. Eat immediately.

VARIATIONS
• Add some garlic or shredded chillies.

• Serve topped with grated Monterey Jack or Cheddar cheese.

• Substitute yoghurt for the soured cream and sliced avocado for the guacamole.

• Drizzle the fajitas with hot sauce.

TANDOORI CHICKEN WITH KACHUMBER

Why not make your own tandoori paste and enjoy a really healthy and delicious dinner, rather than using commercially made paste, which may contain artificial red food colouring made from petroleum? You can marinate the chicken up to 24 hours in advance ready to cook the following day.

SERVES 4 / PREP: 10 MINUTES / CHILL: 30 MINUTES / COOK: 13-15 MINUTES

200g (7oz/scant 1 cup) 0% fat
    Greek yoghurt
2 tbsp ginger paste
3 garlic cloves, crushed
1 tbsp red chilli powder, e.g.
    Kashmiri
2 tsp paprika
1 tsp garam masala
½ tsp ground turmeric
2 tbsp lime or lemon juice
8 chicken drumsticks, skinned
spray oil
fresh coriander (cilantro)
    leaves, for sprinkling
sea salt and freshly ground
    black pepper
boiled rice, to serve

KACHUMBER
16 cherry tomatoes, quartered
½ cucumber, diced
½ red onion, diced
1 green chilli, diced
a small handful of coriander
    (cilantro), finely chopped
¼ tsp ground cumin
juice of 1 lime

1 Mix the yoghurt, ginger paste, garlic, chilli powder, paprika, garam masala, turmeric and lime or lemon juice in a large bowl until you have a spicy red paste.

2 Pat the drumsticks dry with kitchen paper (paper towels) and slash the thickest parts two or three times with a knife. Put them in the paste bowl and coat them all over with the spicy red paste. Cover the bowl and chill them in the fridge for at least 30 minutes.

3 Meanwhile, make the kachumber: mix all the ingredients in a bowl, adding salt and pepper to taste. Cover the bowl and chill it in the fridge until you are ready to serve.

4 Heat the air fryer to 190°C/375°F.

5 Remove the drumsticks from the marinade and lightly spray them with oil. Place them in the basket in a single layer, leaving a little space between them – you may have to cook them in batches depending on the size of your air fryer. Cook them for 13–15 minutes, turning them and spraying them with oil after 6 minutes, until the chicken is cooked through. If you're not sure, pierce the thickest part of a drumstick with a thermometer – it should be 71–75°C (160–165°F).

6 Serve the chicken sprinkled with coriander, with boiled rice and the kachumber salad.

PORK GYROS

Meat or vegetable gyros wrapped in soft pitta breads are traditional Greek street food. They are sometimes served with oregano potato fries, but tzatziki and fresh salad also make excellent accompaniments. Check the labels when buying pittas and flatbreads and choose ones that are wholewheat or wholegrain and high in fibre.

SERVES 4 / PREP: 15 MINUTES / CHILL: 2 HOURS / COOK: 15-20 MINUTES

500g (1lb 2oz) pork tenderloin (fillet), cut into 2cm (¾in) cubes
4 large pitta breads or flatbreads
12 tbsp tzatziki
a few crisp lettuce leaves, shredded
4 ripe tomatoes, sliced or chopped
1 small red onion, thinly sliced
a few sprigs flat-leaf parsley, for sprinkling
smoked paprika, for dusting

MARINADE
3 tbsp olive oil
2 garlic cloves, crushed
1 tsp dried oregano
½ tsp ground cumin
½ tsp ground coriander
½ tsp smoked paprika
½ tsp ground black pepper
½ tsp sea salt

1 Make the marinade: mix all the ingredients in a bowl and then stir in the pork cubes until they are completely coated. Cover the bowl and chill the pork in the fridge for at least 2 hours – or overnight, if you prefer.

2 Heat the air fryer to 180°C/350°F.

3 Thread the pork pieces on to 4 long or 8 short wooden or metal skewers (see tip below). Place them in the air fryer basket in a single layer, leaving a little space between them – you may have to cook them in batches depending on the size of your air fryer. Cook the skewers for 15–20 minutes, turning them once or twice, until the pork is cooked through and golden brown. Test whether the pork is cooked by piercing a piece with a sharp knife. The juices should run clear.

4 Warm the pitta or flatbreads on a hot griddle pan, then spread the tzatziki over them. Remove the pork pieces from the skewers and place them on on top of the tzatziki. Add the lettuce, tomato and onion and sprinkle them with parsley. Dust everything with smoked paprika and roll up the pitta bread into a cone using baking parchment or kitchen foil to hold the filling in place.

5 Serve the gyros immediately and eat them with your fingers.

★ Tip: Soak wooden skewers in a bowl of water for 30 minutes before threading the meat on to them to prevent them burning during cooking.

CRISPY DUCK PANCAKES

Next time you want to eat Chinese crispy duck make it yourself in the air fryer, rather than ordering a takeaway – it's easier than you think. The preparation doesn't take long but it's best to start the day before so you can salt and spice the duck legs and leave them to absorb the flavours overnight.

SERVES 4 / PREP: 15 MINUTES / CHILL: 3 HOURS / COOK: 1-1½ HOURS

4 x 100g (3½oz) free-range duck legs
1 tsp salt
1 tsp whole Sichuan peppercorns, crushed
2 tsp Chinese five-spice powder
2.5cm (1in) piece of fresh root ginger, peeled and grated
2 tbsp Shaoxing wine
16 Chinese pancakes

TO SERVE
½ cucumber, cut into thin matchsticks
1 bunch of spring onions (scallions), white parts only, shredded
hoisin sauce or Szechuan hot plum sauce

★ Tip: Save the duck fat for cooking roast potatoes.

VARIATIONS
• Serve with sweet chilli sauce.
• Try cooking a whole duck rather than just the legs.

1 Prick the duck skin all over with the point of a sharp knife. Mix the salt, peppercorns, five-spice powder, ginger and Shaoxing wine in a bowl. Rub this all over the duck legs, then cover them and chill in the fridge for at least 3 hours or, ideally, overnight.

2 Heat the air fryer to 150°C/300°F.

3 Gently press some kitchen paper (paper towels) on the duck legs to dry them. Place the legs in a single layer in the air fryer basket and cook them for 1 hour, pulling out the basket every 15 minutes or so to drain off the fat. The duck is ready when the skin is crisp and the meat is falling off the bones. If the skin is not crisp enough, cook the legs for 10–20 more minutes.

4 Using two forks, remove the meat and skin from the bones and shred it.

5 Meanwhile, warm the pancakes in a microwave or wrapped in baking parchment or kitchen foil in a steamer set over a saucepan of simmering water.

6 To serve, arrange the duck on a serving platter with the cucumber matchsticks and spring onions on the side. Fill some small individual dishes or ramekins with hoisin or Szechuan hot plum sauce. Keep the pancakes warm in a bamboo steamer basket or cover them with a cloth. Guests can help themselves to pancakes, spread them with sauce, sprinkle them with a little cucumber and spring onions, then top with the duck before folding over or rolling up the pancakes. Enjoy!

GARLIC PRAWNS WITH SPAGHETTI

This is a cheat's shrimp scampi – an Italian classic dish – cooked in the air fryer and then tossed with pasta. If you're using frozen prawns (shrimp), be sure to defrost them thoroughly before cooking.

SERVES 4 / PREP: 5 MINUTES / COOK: 10-12 MINUTES

500g (1lb 2oz) spaghetti or linguine
2 tbsp butter
2 tbsp olive oil
4 garlic cloves, crushed
4 tbsp medium dry white wine
juice of 1 small lemon
a pinch of red pepper flakes
450g (1lb) large raw prawns (jumbo shrimp), shelled and deveined
a small bunch of parsley, chopped
sea salt and freshly ground black pepper

1 Heat the air fryer to 180°C/350°F.

2 Bring a large saucepan of salted water to the boil and cook the pasta according to the packet instructions. Drain well.

3 While the pasta is cooking, put the butter, olive oil and garlic in a 15–18cm (6–7in) pan and place it in the air fryer. Cook for 1 minute, take out the pan, stir and then cook the garlic for 1 more minute.

4 Add the wine, lemon juice and red pepper flakes, and cook for 2 more minutes.

5 Add the prawns and two-thirds of the parsley and cook them for 3–5 minutes, turning the mixture after 2 minutes, until the prawns turn pink and are cooked through. Season them with salt and pepper to taste and stir in the remaining parsley. Set the mixture aside for 1 minute.

6 Toss the pasta in the lemony prawn mixture until it is evenly coated. Divide it between 4 deep pasta dishes and enjoy!

VARIATIONS

• Serve the prawns with some crusty bread – or garlic bread – instead of pasta.

• Use a dry vermouth, such as Noilly Prat or Martini, instead of wine.

• Add some snipped chives.

• For a more intense lemon flavour, add some grated zest and stir in more juice at the end.

★ Tip: If you don't have a small pan that fits inside your air fryer, you could line the basket with kitchen foil, raising the edges to make a container for the prawns and sauce.

MEATBALLS WITH SPAGHETTI

Nearly everyone loves spaghetti and meatballs, especially children, and meatballs are easier and quicker to make in an air fryer than you might think. You don't have to serve them with pasta. They are equally delicious with rice or noodles, or served with a dip as an appetizer.

SERVES 4 / PREP: 15 MINUTES / COOK: 18–22 MINUTES

500g (1lb 2oz/2¼ cups) 20% fat minced (ground) beef
25g (1oz/½ cup) fresh white breadcrumbs
50g (2oz/½ cup) Parmesan, grated
2 garlic cloves, crushed
1 medium free-range egg
1 small onion, grated
a handful of parsley, chopped
4 tbsp olive oil, plus extra for spraying
sea salt and freshly ground black pepper
400g (14oz) spaghetti
grated Parmesan, to serve

EASY TOMATO SAUCE
2 tbsp olive oil
1 onion, diced
3 garlic cloves, crushed
2 x 400g (14oz) tins chopped tomatoes
a pinch of sugar

VARIATIONS
• Use a mixture of minced pork and beef.
• Add some fresh basil leaves to the sauce or use basil as a garnish.

1 Make the tomato sauce: heat the oil in a frying pan (skillet) set over a low to medium heat and cook the onion and garlic for 8–10 minutes until they have softened. Add the tomatoes and sugar and cook them for 10–12 minutes, or until the sauce thickens and reduces. Season with salt and pepper to taste. Remove the sauce from the heat and cover the pan.

2 Meanwhile, make the meatballs: put the mince in a bowl with the breadcrumbs, Parmesan, garlic, egg, onion, parsley, olive oil, salt and pepper. Mix with your hands, scrunching everything together.

3 Take a small piece of the mixture and roll it into a ball a little larger than a walnut but smaller than a golf ball using your hands. Repeat with the remaining mixture so you end up with about 16–20 meatballs.

4 Heat the air fryer to 200°C/400°F.

5 Spray the meatballs with oil and place them in a single layer in the basket, leaving a little space between them – you may have to cook them in batches depending on the size of your air fryer. Cook for 5 minutes, then turn them over and cook them for a further 5–7 minutes until they are browned and cooked through.

6 Meanwhile, cook the spaghetti in a large saucepan of salted water according to the packet instructions. Drain it in a colander, then add it to the sauce and toss until all the strands are well coated. Gently stir in the meatballs.

7 Divide the mixture between 4 shallow bowls and serve immediately, sprinkled with grated Parmesan.

MEXICAN FISH TACOS

Tacos make a quick and easy meal. These are filled with a mixture of spice-rubbed white fish and prawns with added guacamole and spicy pico de gallo or tomato salsa. Fish fillets cook very fast in the air fryer in minimal oil and leave no smell in the kitchen.

SERVES 4 / PREP: 15 MINUTES / COOK: 6-8 MINUTES

450g (1lb) skinned white fish fillets, e.g. cod, haddock, sea bass
spray avocado or olive oil
juice of 1 lime
a handful of coriander (cilantro), chopped
200g (7oz) peeled cooked prawns (shrimp)
8 tortillas
a handful of crisp lettuce leaves, e.g. cos (romaine) or little gem
4 tbsp guacamole
pico de gallo or fiery tomato salsa, for drizzling
sea salt and freshly ground black pepper

SPICY RUB
1 tsp chilli powder
½ tsp smoked paprika
½ tsp garlic powder
¼ tsp ground cumin
¼ tsp cayenne

1. Make the spicy rub: mix all the ingredients in a bowl with plenty of salt and pepper.

2. Pat the fish fillets dry with kitchen paper (paper towels) and then press the spicy rub all over them. Spray them lightly with oil.

3. Heat the air fryer to 200°C/400°F.

4. Place the fish fillets in the air fryer basket in a single layer, leaving a little space between them – you may have to cook them in batches depending on the size of your air fryer. Cook the fillets for 6–8 minutes until they are tender and the fish starts to flake.

5. Cut the fillets into large chunks and sprinkle them with the lime juice and coriander. Add the prawns and season everything lightly with salt and pepper.

6. Warm the tortillas and top with the lettuce, fish, prawns and guacamole. Drizzle with pico de gallo or salsa and fold the tortillas. Serve immediately.

VARIATIONS
- Substitute salmon fillets for white fish.
- Use crisp taco shells instead of tortillas.
- Sprinkle with chopped coriander (cilantro).

JAPANESE BLACK COD

If you love Japanese food, you'll be knocked out by this black cod. You need to prepare the fish a day in advance, so it absorbs the umami flavours of the marinade before you cook it. It's so easy to make and cooks quickly in the air fryer.

SERVES 4 / PREP: 15 MINUTES / MARINATE: OVERNIGHT / COOK: 10-12 MINUTES

4 x 150g (5oz) skinless cod
    fillets, 4cm (1½in) thick
spray oil
300g (10oz) sugar snap peas
    (snow peas)
4 tbsp teriyaki sauce
2 tsp white sesame seeds
2 tsp pickled ginger
2 spring onions (scallions),
    shredded
boiled rice

MARINADE
4 tbsp sake (Japanese rice wine)
4 tbsp mirin
2 tbsp clear honey
1 tbsp dark soy sauce
4 tosp white miso paste

VARIATIONS
• Use sugar instead of honey in the marinade and stir until it dissolves.

• Serve with mangetout or steamed greens.

• Serve with rice noodles drizzled with sesame oil.

---

1   Make the marinade: put the sake, mirin, honey and soy sauce in a small saucepan over a high heat. Stir gently and when it comes to the boil, reduce the heat to low and add the miso paste. Stir until it dissolves and then remove the pan from the heat and set it aside to cool.

2   When the marinade is cold, transfer it to a large container and add the cod fillets, turning them in the miso mixture until they are coated all over. Cover the bowl and chill the fish in the fridge overnight.

3   Heat the air fryer to 180°C/350°F.

4   Remove the fish from the marinade (reserving the marinade) and pat the pieces dry with kitchen paper (paper towels). Lightly spray the air fryer basket with oil and place the cod fillets inside in a single layer. Cook them for 5 minutes, then turn them over and brush them with the leftover marinade. Cook them for a further 5–7 minutes, or until they are glossy brown on the outside and flaky and cooked on the inside.

5   Meanwhile, boil, steam or microwave the sugar snaps until they are just tender. Toss them in the teriyaki sauce and then sprinkle them with sesame seeds.

6   Serve the black cod garnished with the pickled ginger and spring onions, with the sugar snaps and rice.

PIRI PIRI CHICKEN

This fiery Portuguese dish is deservedly popular. You can buy bottles of piri piri sauce and marinade in most supermarkets, but it's more authentic and delicious – and healthier – to make it yourself at home.

SERVES 4 / PREP: 20 MINUTES / MARINATE: 2 HOURS PLUS / COOK: 18-20 MINUTES

leaves stripped from 3 sprigs of thyme
3 red chillies, deseeded and chopped
3 garlic cloves, peeled
2 tsp sweet paprika
1 tbsp red wine vinegar
1 tbsp olive oil
grated zest and juice of 1 small lemon or lime
4 chicken legs (drumsticks and thighs) on the bone, skin on
sea salt and freshly ground black pepper
baked potatoes or rice, to serve

COLESLAW

200g (7oz) white (or mixed red and white) cabbage, thinly shredded
2 large carrots, grated
1 small bunch of spring onions (scallions), chopped
1 red apple, cored and diced
30g (1oz/¼ cup) walnuts, chopped
a handful of parsley, chopped
115g (4oz/½ cup) mayonnaise
juice of ½ small lemon

1 Make the piri piri marinade: pound the thyme leaves, chillies, garlic and sweet paprika to a paste in a pestle and mortar. Stir in the vinegar, olive oil and citrus zest and juice.

2 Put the chicken legs in a bowl and pour over the marinade. Turn the legs in the mixture and then cover and chill them in the fridge for at least 2 hours or, ideally, overnight.

3 Make the coleslaw: mix together the cabbage, carrots, spring onions, apple, walnuts and parsley. Gently stir in the mayonnaise and lemon juice and season to taste with salt and pepper.

4 Heat the air fryer to 190°C/375°F.

5 Line the air fryer basket with kitchen foil. Remove the legs from the marinade and place them in the basket in a single layer. Cook them for 10 minutes and then turn them over. Cook them for a further 8-10 minutes, or until they are crisp and golden brown and cooked through.

6 Serve the chicken legs immediately with the coleslaw and some baked potatoes or rice.

★ Tip: To test whether the chicken is cooked, pierce the thickest part of the leg with a thermometer – it should read 71-75°C/160-165°F. If you don't have a thermometer, pierce a leg with a skewer – the juices should run clear.

FISH FINGERS WITH TARTARE SAUCE

After tasting these crispy fish fingers straight out of the air fryer, you'll never buy supermarket frozen ones again. They are so succulent and flaky and healthier than commercially made ones. Some commercial fish fingers are ultra processed because of the processing methods used to make them and they may contain sugar, palm oil, thickening and raising agents.

SERVES 4 / PREP: 15 MINUTES / COOK: 8-10 MINUTES

600g (1lb 5oz) thick cod fillets, skinned
plain (all-purpose) flour, for dusting
2 medium free-range eggs, beaten
175g (6oz/1½ cups) panko breadcrumbs
spray olive oil
sea salt and freshly ground black pepper
lemon wedges, to serve

TARTARE SAUCE
4 tbsp mayonnaise
1 hard-boiled egg, peeled and chopped
3 gherkins, diced
1 tbsp capers, diced
1 tbsp chopped parsley
a squeeze of lemon juice

1   Make the tartare sauce: put all the ingredients in a bowl and stir gently until they are well combined. Cover the bowl and chill it in the fridge until you are ready to serve.

2   Cut the cod fillets into thick fish-finger size strips and pat them dry with kitchen paper (paper towels). Dust them lightly with flour seasoned with salt and pepper. Dip the strips into the beaten egg and then coat them on both sides with the breadcrumbs.

3   Heat the air fryer to 220°C/425°F.

4   Lightly spray the fish fingers with oil and place them in the air fryer basket in a single layer, leaving a little space between them – you may have to cook them in batches depending on the size of your air fryer. Cook them for 5 minutes, then turn them over and cook them for a further 3–5 minutes, or until they are thoroughly cooked inside and golden and crisp on the outside.

5   Serve them piping hot with the tartare sauce and some lemon wedges for squeezing.

★ Tip: You can check that the fish fingers are cooked through with a meat thermometer – it should read at least 75°C/167°F.

VARIATIONS
• Add some chopped dill to the tartare sauce.
• Serve with garlic mayo (aioli) or tomato ketchup.
• Serve with green beans, peas or French fries (see page 117).
• You can use any firm-fleshed white fish, e.g. haddock, sole or coley.

STUFFED PORK FILLET ROLL

Pork fillet, or tenderloin, is beautifully lean and stays tender and juicy when it's cooked in an air fryer at a high temperature. In this recipe it is stuffed and rolled to make it even more delicious. What's more, it's quick and easy to assemble and cook – and full of protein.

SERVES 4 / PREP: 15 MINUTES / COOK: 15-18 MINUTES

400g (14oz) spinach, trimmed and washed
50g (2oz) sunblush tomatoes, chopped (see note)
150g (5oz) mozzarella, drained and diced
500g (1lb 2oz) pork fillet (tenderloin)
spray oil
sea salt and freshly ground black pepper
brown rice and green beans, to serve

★ Tip: Don't skip resting the meat at the end of cooking – this makes it more succulent and tender.

Note: Sunblush tomatoes are semi-dried and preserved in oil, unlike sun-dried tomatoes, which are often left outside in sunshine until they dry out. Sunblush tomatoes are moister and have a sweeter, intense flavour.

1 Put the spinach leaves in a colander and stand it in the sink. Pour boiling water over the spinach until it wilts and looks bright green. Drain the leaves well, pressing out any excess liquid with a saucer.

2 Pat the spinach dry with kitchen paper (paper towels) and chop it coarsely. Transfer the chopped spinach to a bowl and mix it with the tomatoes and mozzarella. Season with salt and pepper.

3 Use a sharp knife to cut lengthways through the middle of the pork fillet, but don't cut all the way through. This will allow you to open it out flat like a book. Place the fillet between 2 sheets of cling film (plastic wrap) or baking parchment and flatten with a rolling pin.

4 Lay the cut fillet on a clean surface and season it lightly with salt and pepper. Spoon the spinach mixture down the centre and fold the pork over it to enclose the stuffing – you could secure it with wooden toothpicks. Spray the joint lightly with oil.

5 Heat the air fryer to 200°C/400°F.

6 Place the pork in the air fryer basket and cook it for 10 minutes. Turn it over and cook it for a further 5–8 minutes, or until it is cooked through and no longer pink. (You can check it with a meat thermometer – it should read 60°C/140°F.) Remove the pork and set it aside to rest for at least 5 minutes.

7 Carve the pork into thick slices and serve it with nutty brown rice and green beans.

FISH AND CHIPS

Fish and chips are easier to make than you think and take only 30 minutes to cook from start to finish in an air fryer. They are crisp on the outside and deliciously moist and succulent inside – so you won't want to eat supermarket frozen ones again.

SERVES 4 / PREP: 15 MINUTES / COOK: 13-15 MINUTES

4 x 125g (4½oz) skinned white fish fillets, e.g. cod or haddock
50g (2oz/½ cup) plain (all-purpose) flour
2 medium free-range eggs
150g (5oz/1½ cups) panko breadcrumbs
spray oil
sea salt and freshly ground black pepper

TO SERVE
chips or French fries (see pages 116-117)
lemon wedges, malt vinegar, mayonnaise, ketchup

1 Pat the fish fillets dry with kitchen paper (paper towels).

2 Sift the flour into a bowl and season it with salt and pepper. Beat the eggs in a separate bowl. Mix the panko breadcrumbs with some salt and pepper in another bowl.

3 Dip the fish fillets into the flour, shaking off any excess, and then into the beaten egg and finally into the breadcrumbs until they are coated all over. Spray them lightly with oil.

4 Heat the air fryer to 220°C/425°F.

5 Place the fish fillets in the air fryer basket in a single layer with a little space between them – you may have to cook them in batches depending on the size of your air fryer. Cook them for about 7 minutes and then turn them over. Cook them for another 6–8 minutes until they are crisp and golden and the fish flakes easily.

6 Serve the fish hot from the air fryer with chips or French fries, lemon wedges for squeezing and vinegar, mayonnaise or ketchup.

★ Tip: If you have a dual air fryer with 2 baskets you can cook the chips in the crisper basket and the fish in the other basket.

VARIATIONS
• Add some paprika or cayenne to the flour.
• Tartare sauce (see page 90) is a good accompaniment, as are sriracha or wasabi mayo.
• Serve with peas (fresh or frozen).

GREEK HALLOUMI BURGERS

These colourful burgers contain a jackpot of nutrients: protein, essential minerals and vitamins, as well as fibre. You can vary the layers according to what you have in your fridge or kitchen cupboards. If you have an air fryer with a double basket or dual drawers, you can cook the aubergine and halloumi at the same time.

SERVES 4 / PREP: 10 MINUTES / COOK: 16-20 MINUTES

250g (9oz) halloumi, cut into
    4 thick slices
½ tsp dried oregano
½ tsp smoked paprika
olive oil spray
1 round aubergine (eggplant),
    ends trimmed, cut into
    4 thick slices
4 wholegrain burger buns, split
    and toasted
4 heaped tbsp tzatziki
1 ripe avocado, peeled, stoned
    (pitted) and mashed
sea salt and freshly ground
    black pepper
chilli jam or hot sauce, to serve

1   Sprinkle the halloumi slices with the dried oregano and smoked paprika, then spray them lightly with oil.

2   Spray the aubergine slices lightly with oil and season them with salt and pepper.

3   Heat the air fryer to 190°C/375F.

4   Place the aubergine slices in a single layer in the air fryer basket. Cook them for 8–10 minutes until they are tender and golden brown. Keep them warm.

5   Turn up the air fryer to 200°C/400°F.

6   Place the halloumi slices in a single layer in the air fryer basket and cook them for 6 minutes, or until they start to colour. Turn them over and cook for 2–4 minutes more until they are crispy and golden brown.

7   Spread the bases of the burger buns with the tzatziki. Cover them with the aubergine slices and mashed avocado. Top with the halloumi slices and drizzle them with chilli jam or hot sauce. Serve immediately with salad.

VARIATIONS
• Use hummus instead of tzatziki.

• Add a layer of cos (romaine) lettuce and sliced tomatoes.

• Add air-fried red or yellow (bell) peppers or mushrooms.

★ Tip: Instead of burger buns, use split pitta pockets or warmed flatbreads.

CAULIFLOWER CHEESE

Comforting, homely and delicious, there's something special about classic baked cauliflower cheese. Yes, you can cook it in your air fryer and it will be crisp and golden brown on top. Serve it for a light and easy vegetarian supper or as a side dish with steak, roast chicken or beef.

SERVES 3-4 / PREP: 10 MINUTES / COOK: 11-13 MINUTES

75g (3oz/scant ½ cup) butter
50g (2oz/½ cup) plain (all-purpose) flour
600ml (1 pint/2½ cups) milk
200g (7oz/2 cups) grated Cheddar cheese, plus extra for sprinkling
2 tsp English or Dijon mustard
1 cauliflower, trimmed and separated into florets
cayenne pepper, for dusting
sea salt and freshly ground black pepper

VARIATIONS

• Use Caerphilly, Lancashire or Parmesan.

• Try using a small cauliflower plus a head of broccoli divided into florets.

• Sprinkle the top with fresh breadcrumbs and lightly spray it with oil before air frying.

• You can use plant milk, if you like.

1   Make the white sauce: melt the butter in a saucepan over a low heat. Stir in the flour and cook it for 2–3 minutes, continuing to stir until you have a smooth paste. Gradually whisk in the milk a little at a time, beating until it's all added and the sauce is free of lumps. Turn up the heat and bring it to the boil, stirring all the time, until the sauce thickens and coats the back of the spoon – it should be smooth and glossy. Reduce the heat to low and cook the sauce for 2–3 minutes.

2   Take the pan off the heat and stir in the grated Cheddar and mustard. Season the sauce to taste with salt and pepper.

3   Meanwhile, bring a large saucepan of water to the boil and add the cauliflower florets. Boil them for about 6 minutes, or until they are just tender when pierced with a sharp knife. Do not overcook the cauliflower or it will lose its shape and go mushy. Drain the florets well and pat them dry with kitchen paper (paper towels).

4   Arrange the cauliflower in a baking dish that fits your air fryer basket and pour the sauce over the top to cover it completely. Sprinkle it with more grated cheese and dust it with cayenne.

5   Heat the air fryer to 180°C/350°F.

6   Place the cauliflower cheese in the air fryer basket and cook it for 5–7 minutes until it's bubbling, crisp and golden brown on top. Serve immediately.

CHICKEN SATAY

Spicy chicken skewers with satay sauce make an easy supper. You can prepare the satay sauce and the chicken a day ahead of time and leave it to marinate overnight. Serve it with steamed vegetables, such as pak choi, leafy greens or asparagus for a really healthy meal.

SERVES 4 / PREP: 15 MINUTES / MARINATE: 1 HOUR / COOK: 15-19 MINUTES

75ml (3fl oz/generous ¼ cup) coconut milk
1 tsp ground turmeric
1 tsp ground coriander
½ tsp ground cumin
2 garlic cloves, crushed
1 tsp grated fresh root ginger
2 tsp brown sugar
1 tsp soy sauce or nam pla (Thai fish sauce)
a pinch of sea salt
500g (1lb 2oz) skinless chicken breast fillets, cut into 3cm (1¼in) wide strips
spray oil
shredded red chillies and spring onions (scallions), for sprinkling
lime wedges, for squeezing
rice or rice noodles, to serve

SATAY SAUCE
115g (4oz/generous ⅓ cup) crunchy peanut butter
2 tsp Thai red curry paste
300ml (½ pint/1¼ cups) tinned coconut milk
2 tbsp brown sugar
grated zest and juice of 1 lime

1 Make the marinade by mixing together the coconut milk, ground spices, garlic, ginger, sugar, soy sauce and salt in a large bowl.

2 Add the chicken strips to the marinade. Stir gently until all the strips are coated and then cover the bowl and marinate them in the fridge for at least 1 hour.

3 Make the satay sauce: put the peanut butter, curry paste and coconut milk in a saucepan set over a low heat. Stir gently until everything is well blended. Add the sugar and lime juice and simmer gently for 15 minutes, or until the sauce has thickened – if it's too thick, add a little water or more coconut milk. Transfer it to a serving bowl and set it aside to cool slightly.

4 Meanwhile, heat the air fryer to 180°C/350°F.

5 Thread the chicken strips on to 8 wooden, bamboo or metal skewers (see tip on page 79), weaving them through the chicken strips to make 'S' shapes.

6 Lightly spray the air fryer basket with oil and place the skewers inside in a single layer, leaving a little space between them – you may have to cook them in batches depending on the size of your air fryer. Cook the skewers for 5 minutes, then turn them over and cook them for another 5-7 minutes, or until they are golden brown and cooked through.

7 Serve the skewers sprinkled with shredded chillies and spring onions, with the satay sauce, lime wedges and boiled rice.

CRISPY CHILLI BEEF

Everybody loves this as a takeaway from their local Chinese restaurant but you can make a quick and easy – and equally delicious – version in your air fryer at home. To make a really healthy meal, serve the beef with some green vegetables, such as stir-fried broccoli or mangetout.

SERVES 4 / PREP: 15 MINUTES / CHILL: 30 MINUTES / COOK: 6-7 MINUTES

2 tbsp soy sauce
2 tsp sesame oil
1 tsp Chinese five-spice powder
500g (1lb 2oz) lean rump or sirloin steak, sliced into thin strips
4 tbsp cornflour (cornstarch)
spray oil
freshly ground black pepper
a few sprigs of coriander, chopped
rice or noodles, to serve

CHILLI SAUCE
2 tbsp sesame or vegetable oil
4 spring onions (scallions), thinly sliced
2 garlic cloves, crushed
1 red chilli, shredded
2.5cm (1in) piece fresh root ginger, cut into thin matchsticks
1 red (bell) pepper, deseeded and cut into chunks
2 tbsp soy sauce
2 tbsp rice wine vinegar
2 tbsp hot chilli sauce
2 tbsp light brown sugar

1   Mix the soy sauce, sesame oil and five-spice powder in a large bowl. Add a good grinding of pepper and stir in the beef strips. Cover the bowl and chill it in the fridge for 30 minutes.

2   Heat the air fryer to 220°C/425°F.

3   Put the cornflour on a plate and roll the marinated beef strips in it until they are coated. Spray them lightly with oil.

4   Place the beef strips in the air fryer basket in a single layer with a little space between them – you may have to cook them in batches depending on the size of your air fryer. Cook them for 3 minutes and then turn them over and cook them for 2–3 minutes more until they are crisp.

5   Meanwhile, make the chilli sauce: heat the oil in a wok or frying pan (skillet) set over a high heat. Add the spring onions, garlic, chilli, ginger and red pepper and stir-fry them for 3–4 minutes until they are just tender but still crisp. Stir in the remaining ingredients plus 2–3 tablespoons of water and continue to cook until the liquid reduces to a thick and sticky sauce.

6   Add the crispy beef strips and quickly toss everything together. Serve immediately, sprinkled with coriander, with some boiled rice or noodles.

VARIATIONS
• Use sweet chilli sauce instead of sugar.
• Top with shredded chilli and spring onions.

TERIYAKI SALMON PARCELS

Use wild salmon fillets rather than farmed, if you can find them, as wild salmon contains fewer water pollution contaminants. Salmon is one of the most nutritious foods you can eat. It's an excellent source of protein and it's rich in vitamin B12 and omega-3 fatty acids. These promote heart and brain health and support your immune system, so try to eat salmon at least once a week.

SERVES 4 / PREP: 5 MINUTES / CHILL: 15-30 MINUTES / COOK: 6-9 MINUTES

4 skinned salmon fillets
2 tsp toasted sesame seeds
2 spring onions (scallions),
     thinly sliced
boiled rice or noodles, to serve
pak choi (bok choy) or sugar
     snap peas (snow peas),
     to serve

TERIYAKI MARINADE
2 tbsp soy sauce
1 tbsp mirin
1 tbsp clear honey
1 tbsp sweet chilli sauce
1 tsp sesame oil
1 garlic clove, crushed
2.5cm (1in) piece of fresh root
     ginger, peeled and grated

1 Make the marinade: put all the ingredients in a large bowl and mix them well.

2 Pat the salmon fillets dry with kitchen paper (paper towels) and add them to the marinade. Turn them gently until they are completely covered. Chill them in the fridge for 15–30 minutes.

3 Heat the air fryer to 200°C/400°F.

4 Line the air fryer basket with kitchen foil or baking parchment. Place the salmon fillets in the basket in a single layer, leaving a little space between them – you may have to cook them in batches depending on the size of your air fryer. Cook the fillets for 6-9 minutes until they are tender and the flesh starts to flake.

5 Serve the salmon sprinkled with sesame seeds and spring onions with noodles or rice and some green vegetables (pak choi or sugar snap peas) on the side.

⭐ Tip: If you want to be sure the salmon is cooked, insert a meat thermometer – it should read 60–62°C/140–145°F.

VARIATIONS
• Add teriyaki salmon to a rice bowl.
• If you're on a low-carb regime, use cauliflower rice.
• Serve the salmon with asparagus or stir-fried vegetables.
• Use the marinade to cook chicken thighs and breasts.

GARLICKY CHICKEN KYIV

Homemade chicken Kyivs oozing garlicky butter are so superior to the frozen or ready-made ones in supermarket chill cabinets. They are easier to make than you think and very healthy, especially when cooked in the air fryer in minimal oil.

SERVES 4 / PREP: 20 MINUTES / FREEZE: 15-20 MINUTES / COOK: 12-15 MINUTES

4 x 125g (4½oz) skinless chicken breasts
4 tbsp plain (all-purpose) flour, seasoned with salt and pepper
1 medium free-range egg, beaten
175g (6oz/1¾ cups) panko breadcrumbs
spray oil
sea salt and freshly ground black pepper
green salad or green beans, to serve

GARLIC BUTTER
4 tbsp butter, softened
3 garlic cloves, crushed
3 tbsp chopped parsley

VARIATIONS
• Add grated Parmesan or a pinch of paprika to the breadcrumbs.
• Serve with lemon wedges for squeezing or some ketchup.

1 Make the garlic butter: mix together the butter, garlic and parsley in a bowl. Mould it into a cylinder and wrap it tightly in some cling film (plastic wrap). Freeze it for 15–20 minutes, or until frozen.

2 With a sharp knife, cut a horizontal slit in the side of each chicken breast to make a deep pocket.

3 Slice the frozen garlic butter into 4 rounds and place one in each chicken pocket.

4 Dust each chicken breast with seasoned flour and then dip it into the beaten egg before coating it in the panko breadcrumbs.

5 Heat the air fryer to 200°C/400°F.

6 Lightly spray the coated chicken breasts with oil and place them in the air fryer basket in a single layer with a little space between them – you may have to cook them in batches depending on the size of your air fryer. Cook them for 12–15 minutes until they are crisp and golden brown and cooked through. To check, insert a meat thermometer – if the chicken is cooked it should read 75°C/167°F.

7 Let the cooked chicken breasts rest for 5 minutes before serving them, cut into slices or left whole, with some salad or green beans.

★ Tip: If the chicken breasts are very thick, flatten them out a little with a meat tenderizer before stuffing and coating them

SOUTHERN FRIED CHICKEN

The best thing about cooking fried chicken in an air fryer is that it makes the chicken crisp and crunchy on the outside and keeps it juicy inside. It's not oily or greasy and so much healthier than the deep-fried southern chicken sold by fast food outlets.

SERVES 4 / PREP: 15 MINUTES / STAND: 15 MINUTES / COOK: 20-25 MINUTES

150g (5oz/1½ cups) plain (all-purpose) flour
2 tsp paprika
1 tsp dried oregano
1 tsp garlic powder
1 tsp sea salt
½ tsp freshly ground black pepper
240ml (8fl oz/1 cup) buttermilk
2 medium free-range eggs
1kg (2lb 4oz) chicken thighs and drumsticks on the bone
spray avocado or olive oil
hot sauce, for drizzling

1   Mix the flour, paprika, oregano and garlic powder with the salt and pepper in a bowl.

2   In another bowl, beat the buttermilk and eggs until they are well combined.

3   Roll the chicken pieces one by one in the flour, shaking off any excess, and then coat them with the egg and buttermilk mixture before rolling them in the flour again. Place them on a baking sheet and set them aside for 15 minutes before cooking them.

4   Heat the air fryer to 190°C/375°F.

5   Spray the air fryer basket with oil and then lightly spray the chicken pieces all over.

6   Place the chicken pieces in the air fryer basket in a single layer with a little space between them – you may have to cook them in batches depending on the size of your air fryer. Cook them for 15 minutes, then turn the chicken pieces over and cook them for 5-10 more minutes until they are crisp and golden brown and cooked through. To check, insert a meat thermometer – if the chicken is cooked it should read 75°C/167°F.

7   Serve the chicken immediately drizzled with hot sauce, with coleslaw, corn on the cob, potato salad or baked sweet potatoes.

VARIATIONS
• Coat the chicken with panko breadcrumbs instead of flour.

• For spicy chicken, add 1-2 tablespoons of hot sauce to the buttermilk and egg mixture.

INDIAN SPICED TOFU SKEWERS

You can make the spicy tikka marinade for these skewers in advance then assemble and cook them when you get home from work – it's quicker than ordering a takeaway from the local Indian. They are simple, healthy and nutritious, as tofu is a good source of protein and the vegetables and yoghurt marinade contain a jackpot of essential vitamins and minerals.

SERVES 4 / PREP: 20 MINUTES / MARINATE: 2-3 HOURS / COOK: 8-10 MINUTES

400g (14oz) extra-firm tofu,
    pressed (see page 54) and
    cut into 2.5cm (1in) cubes
2 red, green or yellow (bell)
    peppers, deseeded and cut
    into chunks
1 large red onion, cut into
    thin wedges
spray oil
a few sprigs of coriander
    (cilantro), coarsely chopped
boiled rice and mango
    chutney, to serve
coriander and mint
lime wedges, for squeezing

MARINADE
100g (3½oz/½ cup) Greek
    yoghurt
2 garlic cloves, crushed
2 tsp grated fresh root ginger
2 tsp red chilli powder
1 tsp garam masala
1 tsp paprika
a good pinch of salt
juice of ½ lime

1   Make the marinade: mix all the ingredients in a large bowl.

2   Add the tofu cubes to the marinade with the pepper chunks. Stir gently until they are completely coated. Cover and chill the bowl in the fridge for 2–3 hours.

3   Meanwhile, soak 8 bamboo or wooden skewers in cold water for 30 minutes to prevent them burning in the air fryer. You can also use metal skewers.

4   Thread the marinated tofu, peppers and onion alternately on to the skewers. Spray them lightly with oil.

5   Heat the air fryer to 200°C/400°F.

6   Lightly spray the air fryer basket with oil and place the skewers inside in a single layer, leaving a little space between them – you may have to cook them in batches depending on the size of your air fryer. Cook them for 5 minutes, then turn the skewers over and cook them for 3–5 more minutes.

7   Serve the skewers sprinkled with chopped coriander on a bed of boiled rice, with mint and coriander chutney on the side. Squeeze lime juice from the wedges over the skewers.

VARIATIONS
• Serve with coriander and mint or lime chutney.
• Add courgettes and cherry tomatoes to the skewers.
• Substitute fresh paneer for tofu.
• Use ginger and garlic paste instead of fresh.

TEX-MEX VEGGIE TACOS

Warm tacos filled with colourful roasted vegetables and nutritious black beans make a quick and easy supper, especially when you cook the veggies in the air fryer. The beans and cheese are a good source of protein and the vegetables and guacamole count towards your 30 plant foods a week – and boost your intake of dietary fibre and gut health.

SERVES 4 / PREP: 15 MINUTES / COOK: 10-15 MINUTES

1 medium butternut squash, peeled, deseeded and cubed
1 red onion, cut into thin wedges
2 red (bell) peppers, deseeded and cut into chunks
spray olive oil
1 tsp ground cumin
½ tsp chilli powder
1 x 400g (14oz) tin black beans, rinsed and drained
8 small or 4 large corn tortillas, warmed
4 heaped tbsp guacamole
a few sprigs of coriander (cilantro), chopped
75g (3oz/¾ cup) grated Cheddar or Monterey Jack cheese
sea salt and freshly ground black pepper
Greek yoghurt and pico de gallo (or hot salsa), to serve
lime wedges, for squeezing

1 Mix the squash, red onion and pepper pieces in a bowl. Spray them with oil and sprinkle over the spices. Season with salt and pepper and mix everything gently to coat the vegetables.

2 Heat the air fryer to 200°C/400°F.

3 Lightly spray the air fryer basket with oil and add the vegetables in a single layer, with a little space between them – you may have to cook them in batches depending on the size of your air fryer. Cook the vegetables for 10–15 minutes, shaking the basket once or twice, until they are tender inside and crisp and golden on the outside.

4 Mix the roasted vegetables with the black beans and divide the mixture between the tortillas. Top them with the guacamole and sprinkle them with coriander and cheese. Add yoghurt and pico de gallo or let everyone serve themselves.

5 Roll up the tortillas or fold them over to enclose the filling. Serve them immediately with the lime wedges for squeezing.

★ Tip: For the best results, cut the vegetables into similar sized pieces, so they cook evenly.

VARIATIONS

• Add some refried beans or air-fried tofu.

• Use kidney beans instead of black beans and add some sweetcorn kernels.

• Vary the vegetables: try courgettes (zucchini), cauliflower florets and aubergine (eggplant).

TUNA FISHCAKES WITH GARLIC MAYO

Fishcakes are a quick and economical family supper. You will have all or most of the ingredients in your store cupboards and fridge. When buying tinned tuna, look for eco-friendly, line-caught and sustainable fish in spring water rather than oil. Even though it is tinned, it will have been minimally processed and is a very healthy food, rich in protein, vitamins and minerals as well as heart-friendly omega-3 fatty acids.

SERVES 3-4 / PREP: 15 MINUTES / COOK: 11-13 MINUTES

300g (10oz) tinned tuna in spring water, drained
4 spring onions (scallions), shredded or thinly sliced
3 garlic cloves, crushed (minced)
zest and juice of ½ small lemon
a pinch of crushed chilli or red pepper flakes
15g (½oz/¼ cup) fresh breadcrumbs
2 tbsp homemade or good-quality mayonnaise
a few sprigs of flat-leaf parsley, chopped
2 tbsp grated Parmesan (optional)
1 large free-range egg, beaten
100g (3½oz/1 cup) panko breadcrumbs
sea salt and freshly ground black pepper
spray olive oil

GARLIC MAYO
115g (4oz/½ cup) homemade or good-quality mayonnaise
3-4 garlic cloves, peeled and crushed (minced)
1-2 tsp lemon juice

1 Make the garlic mayo: mix the mayonnaise with 3 crushed garlic cloves in a bowl. Taste and add more garlic, if required. Stir in 1 teaspoon lemon juice and taste again, adding more if you wish. Cover the bowl and chill the mayo in the fridge.

2 Lightly flake the drained tuna and place it in a bowl with the spring onions, garlic, lemon zest and juice, chilli or red pepper flakes, breadcrumbs, mayonnaise, parsley and grated Parmesan (if using). Season the mixture with salt and pepper and stir in the beaten egg, until everything is well combined.

3 Divide the mixture into 8 equal-sized portions and shape each into a patty with your hands.

4 Lightly coat the patties on both sides with the panko breadcrumbs, then spray them with oil.

5 Heat the air fryer to 190°C/375°F.

6 Line the air fryer basket with baking parchment. Place the fishcakes inside the basket in a single layer with a little space between them – you may have to cook them in batches depending on the size of your air fryer. Cook them for 8 minutes, then flip them over and lightly spray them with oil. Cook them for a further 3-5 minutes, or until they are golden brown and crispy.

7 Serve the fishcakes immediately with salad or green vegetables and the garlic mayo.

SNACKS & SIDES

Making crisps and dips has never been easier when you cook them in an air fryer. You won't want to buy additive-laden snacks in a supermarket when you can easily create the same crunch and offer your taste buds the same satisfaction with snacks cooked at home. All this is possible without using excessive quantities of oil or any additives. These dishes are packed with flavour and are ideal served alongside a light or main meal – or you can enjoy them on their own as a snack or appetizer.

ZUCCHINI FRIES

Who doesn't like zucchini fries? Deliciously crisp on the outside and tender and juicy inside, they're a great snack – perfect for serving with pre-dinner drinks or as an appetizer. And because they are cooked in the air fryer, you use hardly any oil, making them super healthy.

SERVES 4 / PREP: 15 MINUTES / COOK: 7-10 MINUTES

3 medium courgettes (zucchini), trimmed and cut into 7.5cm (3in) lengths
100g (3½oz/1 cup) panko breadcrumbs
50g (2oz/½ cup) finely grated Parmesan
1 tsp dried oregano or marjoram
50g (2oz/½ cup) plain (all-purpose) flour
2 medium free-range eggs
spray oil
sea salt and freshly ground black pepper

YOGHURT DIP
225g (8oz/1 cup) Greek yoghurt
2 tbsp tahini
2 garlic cloves, crushed
grated zest and juice of ½ lemon
a few sprigs of dill or mint, chopped

1 Pat the courgette pieces dry with kitchen paper (paper towels) to remove any moisture.

2 Mix the panko breadcrumbs, Parmesan and dried herbs in a bowl. Sift the flour into a separate bowl and season it well with salt and pepper. Break the eggs into a third bowl and beat them with a fork or balloon whisk.

3 Heat the air fryer to 200°C/400°F.

4 Dip the courgette pieces in the seasoned flour until they are completely coated, shaking off any excess, and then dip them in the beaten egg. Finally, coat them in the panko breadcrumbs.

5 Lightly spray the air fryer basket with oil and arrange the coated courgettes inside in a single layer with a little space between them – you may have to cook them in batches depending on the size of your air fryer. Cook the courgettes for 7-10 minutes until they are golden brown and crispy on the outside.

6 Meanwhile, mix all the ingredients for the yoghurt dip in a bowl. Serve it with the hot fries.

CRISPY POTATO CHIPS

Freshly cooked chips are delicious and moreish, but they are a hassle to cook at home using a deep fryer or pan. An air fryer simplifies the process, making it quicker, easier and less messy – and the chips are healthier because you use only a fraction of the oil.

SERVES 4 / PREP: 10 MINUTES / SOAK: 10-15 MINUTES / COOK: 20-25 MINUTES

800g (1¾lb) potatoes, e.g. Maris Piper, peeled and cut lengthways into 1cm (½in) thick chips
1 tbsp olive oil
½ tsp sea salt

★ Tip: Soaking the chips before cooking them helps to remove excess starch in the potatoes so the chips cook more evenly and are extra crisp.

1 Place the chips in a bowl of cold water and soak them for 10-15 minutes (see tip below).

2 Drain the potatoes and pat them dry with kitchen paper (paper towels). Put them in a clean, dry bowl and toss them with the oil and sea salt, until they are lightly coated.

3 Heat the air fryer to 190°C/375°F.

4 Place the potatoes in the air fryer basket but don't overcrowd it. Depending on the size of your air fryer, you may need to cook them in batches. Cook them for 15 minutes, shaking the basket once or twice, then flip them over and cook for a further 5-10 minutes, or until they are tender, crisp and golden brown.

FRENCH FRIES

1 Slice the potatoes into thinner fries (about half the thickness of chips), then soak, pat dry and toss them in seasoned oil as opposite.

2 Cook them for 10 minutes, then shake them well and cook them for 10 more minutes, or until they are crisp and golden.

SWEET POTATO FRIES

1 Peel 2 medium to large sweet potatoes and cut them lengthways into 1cm (½in) thick chips (as above).

2 Toss them in olive oil, smoked paprika, sea salt and chilli powder (optional).

3 Cook them at 190°C/375°F for 10–12 minutes, shaking the basket occasionally.

VARIATIONS

• Alternatively, make chips from swede (rutabaga), butternut squash or plantain.

• Toss the chips or fries in olive oil with some dried oregano or thyme, ground black pepper or sweet paprika.

• Serve the fries with tomato ketchup, mayonnaise or tartare sauce (see page 90).

HOMEMADE VEGGIE CRISPS

These veggie crisps won't last long – once everyone digs in they'll soon disappear. Make them in the air fryer rather than deep-frying them – it's simple and clean. This is a great way to use the root vegetables lurking at the back of your fridge. It's easiest to slice vegetables very thinly with a mandoline if you have one. These crisps are much cheaper and healthier than a ready-made packet bought in the supermarket.

SERVES 4 / PREP: 15 MINUTES / COOK: 15-20 MINUTES

450g (1lb) root vegetables, e.g. sweet potato, beetroot (beets), parsnips, swede (rutabaga), carrots, washed, peeled and very thinly sliced
2 tsp cornflour (cornstarch)
2 tbsp olive oil
½-1 tsp sea salt
1 tsp smoked paprika
freshly ground black pepper

1 Pat the vegetable slices dry with kitchen paper (paper towels). Put them into a large bowl and dust them with the cornflour, tossing them gently so they are evenly coated.

2 Pour over the olive oil and toss the slices in it – then sprinkle over the sea salt, smoked paprika and pepper and toss them again.

3 Heat the air fryer to 170°C/325°F.

4 Place the sliced vegetables in the basket in a single layer – you may have to cook them in batches depending on the size of your air fryer. Cook them for 15-20 minutes, shaking the basket at 5-minute intervals, and checking them frequently, until they are crisp.

5 Once cool, you can store the crisps in an airtight container at room temperature for up to 3 days.

★ Tip: If you use sweet potatoes, soak the slices in cold water for 30 minutes and then dry them with kitchen paper (paper towels) before tossing them in the cornflour, olive oil and spices. Soaking removes starch and makes them crisper.

VARIATIONS
• Add a sprinkling of dried oregano or thyme.
• Vary the spices: try paprika, cumin or chilli powder.
• Sprinkle with garlic powder.
• Sprinkle with truffle salt or spray with truffle oil.

MOZZARELLA FRIES

You will need a block of mozzarella to make these fries. A block contains less moisture than mozzarella balls, which are packed in whey. These fries are crispy on the outside and wonderfully gooey inside – and are sure to be a hit!

SERVES 4-6 / PREP: 15 MINUTES / COOK: 5-8 MINUTES

400g (14oz) block mozzarella, cut into 1cm (½in) fingers
50g (2oz/½ cup) plain (all-purpose) flour
1 tsp garlic powder
1 tsp Italian seasoning
1 tsp dried marjoram or oregano
3 medium free-range eggs
200g (7oz/2 cups) panko breadcrumbs
spray oil
sea salt and freshly ground black pepper
sweet chilli sauce, for drizzling (optional)

1 Heat the air fryer to 220°C/425°F. Line a baking tray with baking parchment.

2 Gently pat the mozzarella fingers dry with kitchen paper (paper towels).

3 Sift the flour into a bowl and stir in the garlic powder, Italian seasoning and herbs. Season with plenty of salt and pepper. Whisk the eggs in another bowl, and put the breadcrumbs into a third bowl.

4 Dip each mozzarella finger in the flour, shaking off any excess, and then into the beaten egg before coating it with breadcrumbs. Place the coated fingers on the lined baking tray. Lightly spray them with oil.

5 Lightly spray the air fryer basket with oil and place the mozzarella fingers inside in a single layer with a little space between them – you may have to cook them in batches depending on the size of your air fryer. Cook the fingers for 5–8 minutes until they are golden brown and crispy on the outside.

6 Serve the mozzarella fries piping hot with a drizzle of sweet chilli sauce.

★ Tip: To prevent the mozzarella fries sticking, you can line the basket with baking parchment.

VARIATIONS
• Use Cajun seasoning or smoked paprika for a spicier coating.
• Serve with pesto, aioli or some tomato ketchup.

CRISPY SPRING ROLLS

Why not make your own air fryer spring rolls with the minimum of oil, rather than heating up frozen supermarket spring rolls or ordering a takeaway? They taste fabulous and they're wonderfully golden and crisp. In fact, they're so good that you may want to double the quantity and cook them in two batches.

SERVES 4 / PREP: 15 MINUTES / COOK: 10-15 MINUTES

1 large carrot, cut into thin matchsticks
1 red or yellow (bell) pepper, deseeded and thinly sliced
2 spring onions (scallions), thinly sliced
225g (8oz) peeled cooked prawns (shrimp)
a few sprigs of coriander (cilantro), chopped
a few drops of dark soy sauce
4 rice paper wrappers
spray oil
sweet chilli sauce, for dipping

VARIATIONS

• Use shredded cooked chicken or turkey instead of prawns.

• For vegetarian spring rolls, omit the prawns and add some beansprouts and shredded spring greens or kale to the filling.

• Serve with satay sauce, hoisin sauce or any hot sauce.

1 Mix together the carrot, pepper, spring onions, prawns and coriander in a bowl. Drizzle a little soy sauce over them and stir well.

2 Fill a bowl with tepid water and position it near you while you assemble the spring rolls. Dip a rice paper wrapper in the water for a minute or two until it becomes pliable, then lay it flat on a clean work surface.

3 Spoon a quarter of the prawn and vegetable mixture on to the wrapper, leaving a wide edge around the filling.

4 Fold the sides of the wrapper over the filling to enclose it and then roll it up like a parcel. Repeat with the rest of the wrappers and filling. Brush the spring rolls lightly with oil.

5 Heat the air fryer to 200°C/400°F and line the basket with baking parchment.

6 Place the spring rolls in the basket seam-side down in a single layer with a little space between them. Cook them for 10-15 minutes until they are crispy and golden. Serve them piping hot with sweet chilli sauce.

★ Tip: If the prawns are large cut them into smaller pieces.

HALLOUMI FRIES WITH WATERMELON SALSA

Healthy, salty and delicious, halloumi has become one of the world's most popular cheeses. What makes it special is its high melting point, which means you can grill, griddle, fry or bake it without it melting or losing its shape. Better still, it cooks amazingly well in an air fryer, too!

SERVES 4 / PREP: 20 MINUTES / COOK: 6-8 MINUTES

350g (12oz) halloumi,
   sliced lengthwise into
   thick fingers
25g (1oz/¼ cup) plain
   (all-purpose) flour
1 tsp ground cumin
1 tsp dried oregano
spray oil
sea salt and freshly ground
   black pepper

WATERMELON SALSA
300g (10oz) watermelon, rind
   removed, flesh diced and
   seeded
4 spring onions (scallions),
   diced
1 red chilli, diced
a handful of coriander
   (cilantro), chopped
2 tbsp olive oil
grated zest and juice of 1 lime
clear Greek honey (optional)

1   Make the watermelon salsa: put all the ingredients in a bowl and mix them well. Sweeten the salsa with some Greek honey (if using). Cover the bowl and chill it in the fridge while you make the fries.

2   Preheat the air fryer to 180°C/350°F.

3   Pat the halloumi slices dry with kitchen paper (paper towels). Sift the flour into a bowl and stir in the cumin, oregano and some salt and pepper.

4   Lightly toss the halloumi fingers in the seasoned flour until they are well coated and then spray them lightly with oil.

5   Place them in the air fryer in a single layer with a little space between each – you may have to cook them in batches depending on the size of your air fryer. Cook the halloumi fingers for 4 minutes, then turn them over and cook them for another 2–4 minutes until they are golden and crisp.

6   Serve the fries immediately with the watermelon salsa, or your favourite dip.

SPICY CHICKPEAS

These crunchy chickpeas are great to munch and make a nutritious high-fibre snack or a topping for soups and salads. If you can resist eating them in one session, they will stay fresh stored in an airtight container at room temperature for a week. Experiment with different spice combos to discover your favourite flavour.

SERVES 3-4 / PREP: 5 MINUTES / COOK: 10-12 MINUTES

1 x 400g (14oz) tin chickpeas (garbanzo beans), drained and rinsed
2 tsp olive oil
½ tsp garlic powder
¼ tsp cayenne pepper or chilli powder
¼ tsp ground cumin
sea salt and freshly ground black pepper
chopped coriander (cilantro), chives or parsley, to serve (optional)

1 Heat the air fryer to 200°C/400°F.

2 Pat the chickpeas dry with kitchen paper (paper towels) and then place them in a bowl with the oil, spices and salt and pepper. Toss or stir them gently until the chickpeas are coated all over.

3 Place the chickpeas in the air fryer basket, taking care not to overcrowd them. They should be in a single layer with a little space between each one – you may have to cook them in batches. Cook them for 10–12 minutes, shaking the basket every 4–5 minutes, until they are crisp and golden brown.

4 Set the chickpeas aside to cool before serving. Sprinkle the chopped coriander (cilantro), chives or parsley over them (if using).

VARIATIONS
• Add a dash of lemon juice or sriracha before air frying.

• Vary the spice combos: try ground cinnamon, coriander, smoked paprika, allspice or za'atar.

• After 10 minutes cooking, grate some Parmesan over the chickpeas then replace them in the air fryer for 2 minutes.

NUTTY TRAIL MIX

Enjoy this trail mix as a high-energy snack or sprinkle it over your breakfast cereal – or use it as a crunchy topping for yoghurt and smoothie bowls. Use shelled raw nuts rather than salted, roasted or candied ones.

SERVES 3-4 / PREP: 5 MINUTES / COOK: 6-8 MINUTES

150g (5oz/generous 1 cup) mixed shelled
    nuts, e.g. almonds, cashews, pistachios
25g (1oz/scant ¼ cup) raisins
2 tbsp mixed seeds, e.g. sunflower, pumpkin, sesame
25g (1oz/generous ¼ cup) coconut flakes
½ tsp sea salt
1 tbsp maple syrup
a few drops of vanilla extract
1 tbsp coconut oil, melted

1. Heat the air fryer to 180°C/350°F. Line the basket with some baking parchment.

2. Put all the ingredients in a bowl and stir them well until everything is lightly coated with the maple syrup and coconut oil.

3. Transfer the mixture to the lined air fryer basket and cook it for 3 minutes, then shake the basket or stir the mixture. Cook it for 3–5 minutes more, checking once or twice, until the nuts are evenly browned but not too dark.

4. Remove the basket and leave the mixture to cool. Store the trail mix in an airtight container in a cool dry place. It will keep well for up to 2 weeks.

VARIATIONS
- Use agave syrup or clear honey instead of maple syrup.
- Substitute sultanas (golden raisins) for the raisins.
- Stir some dried cranberries or dark chocolate chips into the cooled trail mix.

BUFFALO CAULI BITES

This buffalo cauli is crisper and tastier than most versions because the cauliflower florets are coated with crunchy golden panko crumbs. You can serve them with a classic buffalo sauce or ranch dressing or just a squeeze of lemon juice.

SERVES 4 / PREP: 15 MINUTES / COOK: 10-12 MINUTES

50g (2oz/½ cup) plain (all-purpose) flour
1 tsp ground cumin
1 tsp sweet smoked paprika
½ tsp garlic powder
3 medium free-range eggs
200g (7oz/2 cups) panko breadcrumbs
1 medium cauliflower, leaves and stem removed, divided into bite-sized florets
spray oil
sea salt and freshly ground black pepper

BUFFALO SAUCE
120ml (4fl oz/½ cup) red hot sauce, e.g. Tabasco
50g (2oz/¼ cup) butter
1 tbsp clear honey
a few drops of Worcestershire sauce (optional)
½ tsp paprika
½ tsp garlic powder

⭐ Tip: When coating the cauliflower, use one hand to coat the florets with the dry ingredients (flour and breadcrumbs) and the other hand to dip them into the beaten egg.

1 Make the buffalo sauce: put all the ingredients in a saucepan and season them with salt and pepper. Set the pan over a low to medium heat and simmer the sauce gently, stirring all the time until the butter melts and the sauce starts to bubble. Remove the pan from the heat and set it aside while you prepare the cauliflower bites.

2 Sift the flour into a bowl and stir in the ground spices and garlic powder. Beat the eggs in a separate bowl. Put the panko breadcrumbs and salt and pepper into a third bowl.

3 Bring a saucepan of salted water to the boil and tip in the florets. Cook them for 3 minutes until they are just tender but still firm. Drain them in a colander and then refresh them in cold water. Finally, pat them dry with kitchen paper (paper towels).

4 Heat the air fryer to 180°C/350°F.

5 Toss the cauliflower florets in the flour, shaking off any excess, and then dip them in the beaten egg before coating them with the panko breadcrumbs.

6 Spray the coated florets lightly with oil and place them in the air fryer basket in a single layer with a little space between them – you may have to cook them in batches depending on the size of your air fryer. Cook them for 6 minutes and then turn them over. Cook them for a further 4–6 minutes until they are golden brown and crispy.

7 Meanwhile, warm the buffalo sauce and drizzle it over the cauliflower bites, or serve it separately as a dip.

CRISPY ONION RINGS

Serve these onion rings as an accompaniment to steaks, sausages and burgers, or as dippers with tzatziki, tartare sauce, ketchup or mayo. They are meltingly sweet and tender inside and deliciously crisp outside – and cooking them in the air fryer makes them better for you and less oily.

SERVES 3-4 / PREP: 15 MINUTES / COOK: 8-12 MINUTES

50g (2oz/¼ cup) plain (all-purpose) flour
½ tsp garlic powder
pinch of cayenne pepper
2 medium free-range eggs
100g (3½oz/1 cup) panko breadcrumbs
1 large white onion, cut into 1cm (½in) slices and separated into rings
spray olive oil
sea salt and freshly ground black pepper

1   Mix the flour, garlic powder, cayenne and some salt and pepper in a shallow bowl. Beat the eggs in another bowl. Put the panko breadcrumbs with some salt and pepper in a third bowl.

2   Dip the onion rings into the flour and then the beaten egg. Coat them with the breadcrumbs and spray them lightly with olive oil.

3   Heat the air fryer to 190°C/375°F. Line the air fryer basket with baking parchment.

4   Put the onion rings in the basket in a single layer with a little space between them – you may have to cook them in batches depending on the size of your air fryer. Cook them for 8-12 minutes until they are golden brown and crispy.

VARIATIONS
• Add some smoked paprika or chilli powder to the flour mix.

• You can use cornflour (cornstarch) instead of regular flour.

• Use regular breadcrumbs instead of panko, although they won't be so crisp.

ONION BHAJIS

Homemade crisp onion bhajis are a wonderful treat. Serve them as part of an Indian-themed dinner or as a snack or party food. They are surprisingly easy to make and cooking them in an air fryer is less messy than deep-frying them.

SERVES 4-6 / PREP: 10 MINUTES / COOK: 9-11 MINUTES

75g (3oz/scant 1 cup)
    chickpea (gram) flour
1 tsp turmeric
1 tsp ground cumin
1 tsp ground coriander
1 tsp chilli powder
1 tsp garlic paste
a good pinch of sea salt, plus
    extra for sprinkling
a handful of coriander
    (cilantro), chopped
cold water, to mix
2 onions, thinly sliced
¼ tsp bicarbonate of soda
    (baking soda)
spray oil
mango chutney or raita,
    to serve

1   Put the flour, ground spices, garlic paste, salt and chopped coriander in a bowl. Mix well and then whisk in just enough cold water to bind everything together and make a thick batter (similar in consistency to thick Greek yoghurt).

2   Gently stir the sliced onions into the batter until they are coated all over and then stir in the bicarbonate of soda.

3   Divide the mixture into 12 equal portions and mould each into a ball with your hands, flattening them slightly. Lightly spray the bhajis with oil.

4   Heat the air fryer to 190°C/375°F.

5   Spray the air fryer basket with oil and put in the bhajis in a single layer with a little space between them – you may have to cook them in batches depending on the size of your air fryer. Cook them for 5 minutes, then flip them over and spray them lightly with oil. Return them to the air fryer and cook them for 4–6 more minutes until they are crisp and golden brown.

6   Eat the bhajis piping hot. Sprinkle them with sea salt, and serve them with mango chutney or raita on the side.

VARIATIONS
• Serve with Indian pickles or cucumber raita flavoured with mint.

• Add a teaspoon of fennel seeds and a diced fresh chilli to the batter.

★ Tip: The batter must be thick, not soft or runny, or the bhajis won't hold their shape.

PANKO PRAWNS WITH LEMON MAYO

The contrast between the juicy tender prawns and their crisp panko coating makes this recipe extra delicious. Serve the prawns as an appetizer or a snack with pre-dinner drinks. A tart lemon mayo is the perfect dip.

SERVES 4 / PREP: 15 MINUTES / COOK: 5-8 MINUTES

50g (2oz/½ cup) plain
    (all-purpose) flour
2 medium free-range eggs
200g (7oz/2 cups) panko
    breadcrumbs
20 large raw prawns (shrimp),
    peeled and deveined
spray oil
sea salt and freshly ground
    black pepper
lemon wedges, to serve

LEMON MAYO
115g (4oz/½ cup) good-quality
    mayonnaise
grated zest and juice
    of ½-1 lemon

1   Make the lemon mayo: blend the mayonnaise with the lemon zest and juice. Taste and add more lemon if you like it very lemony. Cover the mayo and chill it in the fridge while you prepare and cook the prawns.

2   Sift the flour into a bowl. Beat the eggs in a separate bowl. Put the panko breadcrumbs into a third bowl and season with salt and pepper.

3   Heat the air fryer to 200°C/400°F.

4   Pat the prawns dry with kitchen paper (paper towels) and dip them in the flour, shaking off any excess. Dip them in the beaten egg before rolling them in the breadcrumbs. Spray them lightly with oil.

5   Lightly spray the air fryer basket with oil and add the prawns in a single layer with a little space between them – you may have to cook them in batches depending on the size of your air fryer. Cook the prawns for 5–8 minutes until they are crisp and golden.

6   Serve them immediately with lemon wedges for squeezing and the lemon mayo for dipping.

VARIATIONS
• Serve with aioli (garlic mayo), tartare sauce (see page 90) or sweet chilli sauce.
• Dip the hot prawns into a bowl of coconut yoghurt flavoured with grated lime zest and chopped coriander (cilantro).
• Serve in a basket with some hot potato fries.

CRISPY BUFFALO WINGS

There's no need to order an expensive takeaway when you can make excellent crispy buffalo wings in your air fryer – and there's no mess and minimal washing up. Serve these as snacks, as part of a buffet or with a salad for supper.

SERVES 4-6 / PREP: 10 MINUTES / COOK: 20-25 MINUTES

900g (2lb) free-range or
    organic chicken wings
1 tsp sea salt
½ tsp ground black pepper
spray oil
snipped chives or spring
    onions (scallions), to serve

BUFFALO SAUCE
120ml (4fl oz/½ cup) red hot
    sauce, e.g. Frank's
45g (1½oz/3 tbsp) butter,
    melted
1 tbsp clear honey
1 tbsp white vinegar
1 tsp Worcestershire sauce
    (optional)
½ tsp garlic powder

1   Heat the air fryer to 190°C/375°F.

2   Separate each chicken wing into 2 pieces (known as drumettes and flats) if the butcher hasn't already done so. Pat the pieces dry with kitchen paper (paper towels) – this helps the skin to crisp well. Put them into a large bowl and toss them in the sea salt and black pepper.

3   Lightly spray the air fryer basket with oil and add the chicken pieces in a single layer. Depending on the size of your air fryer you may have to cook them in batches.

4   Cook them for 10 minutes, then turn them over and cook them for a further 10–15 minutes until they are crispy and golden brown.

5   While they are cooking make the buffalo sauce: put all the ingredients into a bowl and whisk them until you have a smooth and well combined sauce.

6   Transfer the cooked wings to a bowl and toss them in the sauce. Sprinkle them with chives or spring onions and serve immediately.

⭐ Tip: To make the wings super crisp, increase the heat to 200°C/400°F at the end of step 4 and cook them for another 4–5 minutes.

VARIATIONS
• You can rub the wings with herbs and spices (dry rub) before air frying them. Try a combo of garlic powder, smoked paprika and dried thyme or oregano.

• Serve the wings with some ranch or blue cheese dressing for dipping.

CHEESY CHILLI BROCCOLI

Even people who don't like broccoli enjoy this. It's crisp, cheesy and delicious – and a great way to tempt children to eat a green vegetable. What's more, it's quick and easy to cook in your air fryer.

SERVES 3-4 / PREP: 10 MINUTES / COOK: 4-7 MINUTES

1 large broccoli head with
 a thick stem
3 tbsp olive oil
3 garlic cloves, crushed
1 red chilli, finely chopped
4 tbsp grated Parmesan, plus
 extra for sprinkling
sea salt and freshly ground
 black pepper

Note: If you can't get broccoli with a thick stem, separate it into even-sized florets and toss them in the cheesy chilli oil, then cook them in the air fryer in the same way.

1 Trim the end of the broccoli stem and then slice the head into large florets with part of the stem attached.

2 Mix the oil, garlic, chilli and Parmesan in a shallow bowl. Season with salt and pepper and add the broccoli pieces, turning them in the oil until they are coated all over.

3 Heat the air fryer to 190°C/375°F.

4 Lightly spray the air fryer basket with oil and add the broccoli pieces in a single layer. Depending on the size of your air fryer, you may need to cook them in batches. Cook them for 4–7 minutes, shaking the basket once or twice, or until they are slightly charred, crisp and tender.

5 Serve immediately, sprinkled with more Parmesan.

★ Tip: You could use tenderstem (longstem) broccoli instead of calabrese and trim the stems before coating them with oil.

VARIATIONS
• Use crushed chilli flakes instead of fresh chilli.
• Substitute garlic salt for fresh garlic.
• If you don't have Parmesan, use Cheddar or Pecorino.

GREEN FALAFELS WITH TAHINI DRIZZLE

These falafels surprise you when you bite into them and discover the bright green interior. Packed with fresh herbs and spices, they taste and look delicious, and they are crisp on the outside and moist inside.

SERVES 4 / PREP: 20 MINUTES / CHILL: 30 MINUTES (OPTIONAL) / COOK: 10-15 MINUTES

400g (14oz/1½ cups) tinned chickpeas (garbanzo beans), drained and rinsed
4 spring onions (scallions), sliced
3 garlic cloves, crushed
a bunch of coriander (cilantro), coarsely chopped
a bunch of flat-leaf parsley, coarsely chopped
a handful of mint, coarsely chopped
1 tbsp chickpea (gram) flour
½ tsp baking powder
½ tsp sea salt
1 tsp ground cumin
1 tsp ground coriander
freshly ground black pepper
spray oil
chilli flakes, to serve (optional)

TAHINI DRIZZLE
1-2 garlic cloves, crushed
a pinch of sea salt
2 tbsp tahini
juice of ½ lemon
100g (3½oz/scant ½ cup) Greek yoghurt

1   Make the tahini drizzle: put all the ingredients into a small bowl and mix well. If the mixture is too thick to drizzle, thin it with cold water.

2   Pat the chickpeas dry with kitchen paper (paper towels). Blitz them with the spring onions, garlic and herbs in a food processor. Add the chickpea flour, baking powder, sea salt, ground spices and black pepper. Pulse, scraping the sides of the food processor occasionally, until everything is well combined and the mixture holds together. If the mixture is too dry and falls apart, add 1-3 tablespoons of cold water. Take care not to overprocess the mixture – the texture should be coarse.

3   Divide the mixture into 8 equal portions and shape each one into a ball, flattening the balls slightly with your hands. You can chill them in the fridge for 30 minutes to make them firmer, but this is not essential.

4   Preheat the air fryer to 190°C/375°F.

5   Lightly spray the falafels with oil and place them in the air fryer basket in a single layer with a little space between them – you may have to cook them in batches depending on the size of your air fryer. Cook them for 10 minutes and if they are not crisp and golden brown, cook them for another 3–5 minutes.

6   Serve the hot falafels with the tahini drizzle, scattered with chilli flakes (if using).

BABA GANOUSH

This smoky aubergine purée is served throughout the Levant, Greece, Turkey and Egypt. There are many variations but this is the classic dish. Serve it as a snack, appetizer or as part of a meze spread with warm pitta triangles, flatbreads or raw vegetables for dipping.

SERVES 4 / PREP: 10 MINUTES / DRAIN: 15 MINUTES / COOK: 15-20 MINUTES

2 medium aubergines (eggplants), sliced in half lengthways
4 tbsp olive oil, plus extra for drizzling
2 garlic cloves, crushed
juice of 1 small lemon
a few sprigs of flat-leaf parsley or mint, chopped
sea salt and freshly ground black pepper
pomegranate seeds, for sprinkling
warm pitta triangles or flatbreads, to serve

1   Heat the air fryer to 200°C/400°F.

2   Sprinkle the cut sides of the aubergine with salt and drizzle them with 2 tablespoons of the olive oil. Cook them in the air fryer for 15 minutes, or until they are so soft that they lose their shape and start to collapse. If they are still a bit firm, cook them for another 5 minutes.

3   Scoop the soft flesh into a sieve set over a bowl. Leave it for 15 minutes to allow any excess liquid to drain away.

4   Transfer the flesh to a bowl and mash it with a fork. Stir in the garlic, lemon juice, the remaining olive oil and the herbs. Season to taste with salt and pepper

5   Serve the baba ganoush drizzled with olive oil and sprinkled with pomegranate seeds, with warm pitta triangles or flatbreads.

★ Tip: For a really smooth purée blitz everything in a food processor – but it's more authentic to mash the aubergine flesh with a fork.

VARIATIONS
• Add 2 tablespoons of tahini.

• Add a pinch of smoked paprika or some toasted cumin seeds.

• Use coriander (cilantro) instead of parsley or mint, or sprinkle it over the top.

• Scatter with red pepper flakes or even crumbled feta.

SPEEDY GARLIC BREAD

This is as good as it gets. A garlic baguette is quick and easy to make and you don't need lots of ingredients. Serve it as a late-night snack, at parties and barbecues, or an accompaniment to soup. You'll never grow tired of it.

SERVES 4-6 / PREP: 10 MINUTES / COOK: 15 MINUTES

125g (4½oz/generous ½ cup) butter, softened
4-5 garlic cloves, crushed
a handful of flat-leaf parsley, chopped
a pinch of red pepper or chilli flakes (optional)
1 crusty baguette (French stick)
sea salt and freshly ground black pepper

1 Put the softened butter in a bowl with the garlic and parsley. Mix well to distribute the garlic and herbs through the butter. Add the red pepper or chilli flakes (if using) and sea salt and pepper to taste. If you are using salted butter, don't add salt.

2 Cut the baguette in half, so the two halves will fit the air fryer basket. If the basket is quite small, you may have to cut the baguette into three sections.

3 Now make vertical cuts about 2cm (¾in) apart almost all the way through the baguette pieces. Take care not to slice through the bottom.

4 Smear most of the garlic butter into the cuts and the remainder over the top. Wrap each section of baguette in kitchen foil.

5 Heat the air fryer to 200°C/400°F.

6 Place the foil-wrapped bread in the air fryer and cook it for 15 minutes, or until the crust starts to crisp and it's oozing with melted butter. Tear it apart and share!

VARIATIONS
• Vary the herbs: try coriander (cilantro), thyme or basil.
• Add a little shredded mozzarella or grated Parmesan or Cheddar to the cuts in the baguette.
• You can reduce or increase the number of garlic cloves you use depending on how much you like garlic.

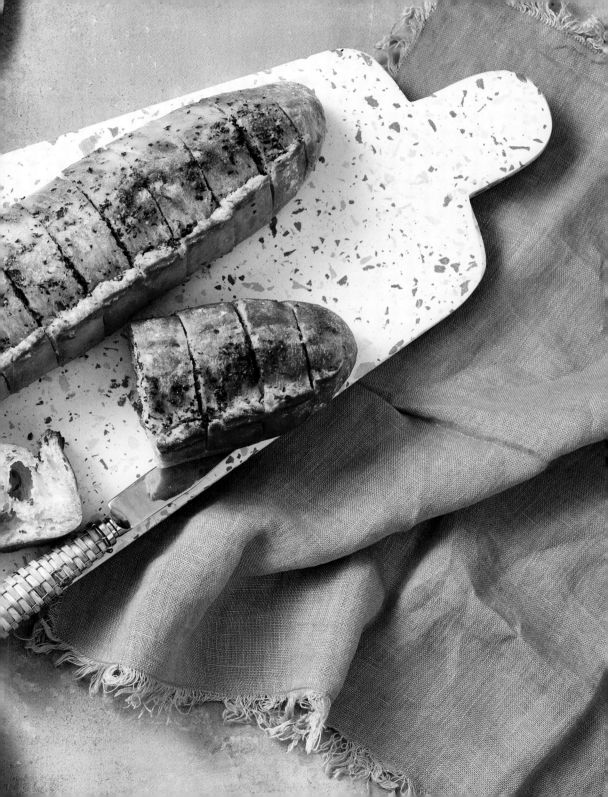

VEGGIE TEMPURA WITH OUZO MAYO

Tempura make a great snack or appetizer – or even a vegetable side with rice and noodle dishes. The key to making successful tempura in an air fryer is to use a thick batter, so it's crisp and lacy and clings to the tender vegetables. Using vegan mayo instead of eggs in the batter makes this vegan-friendly.

SERVES 3-4 / PREP: 15 MINUTES / COOK: 7-10 MINUTES

spray oil
50g (2oz/½ cup) plain
    (all-purpose) flour
sea salt
1 aubergine (eggplant),
    trimmed and thinly sliced
2 courgettes (zucchini),
    trimmed and thinly sliced

OUZO MAYO
225g (8oz/1 cup) vegan
    mayonnaise
2 tbsp ouzo
a small handful of dill, finely
    chopped

BATTER
50g (2oz/½ cup) plain
    (all-purpose) flour
2 tbsp good-quality vegan
    mayonnaise
120ml (4fl oz/½ cup) cold water
sea salt and freshly ground
    black pepper

1 Make the ouzo mayo: put the mayonnaise in a bowl and stir in the ouzo and dill. Cover and chill in the fridge.

2 Make the batter: beat the flour, mayonnaise and cold water until you have a stiff batter. Don't overmix – the batter does not need to be smooth and completely lump-free. Beat in some salt and pepper to season.

3 Heat the air fryer to 180°C/350°F. Lightly spray the basket with oil.

4 Put the flour in a shallow bowl and mix in a good pinch of sea salt. Dip the aubergine and courgette slices into the batter and then into the seasoned flour. Lightly spray them with oil.

5 Place the vegetables in the air fryer basket in a single layer – you may have to cook them in batches depending on the size of your air fryer. Cook them for 7-10 minutes until they are crisp and golden.

6 Sprinkle the hot tempura with sea salt and serve them immediately with the ouzo mayo.

VARIATIONS
• Try other vegetables: red and yellow (bell) peppers, cauliflower, mushrooms and broccoli florets.
• Substitute large prawns (shrimp) for the vegetables.
• Serve with wasabi mayo – stir 1 teaspoon wasabi paste into a cup of mayo.

TORTILLA CHIPS

It's easy to make crispy golden tortilla chips in an air fryer and much cheaper than buying a packet in the supermarket. Homemade tortilla chips are also natural and healthy and contain no additives. Serve them with a spicy Mexican dip, such as hot salsa (pico de gallo) or guacamole.

SERVES 4-6 / PREP: 10 MINUTES / COOK: 6-9 MINUTES

1 tbsp olive or avocado oil
¼ tsp sea salt
6 yellow corn tortillas
   (not large wraps)

FLAVOURINGS
choose from the following:
1 tsp smoked paprika
1 tsp chilli powder
1 tsp ground turmeric
½ tsp garlic powder
½ tsp onion powder
½ tsp ground chipotle chilli
   pepper

1 Heat the air fryer to 180°C/350°F.

2 In a small bowl, whisk together the oil, salt and flavouring(s) of your choice. Lightly brush the flavoured oil over both sides of the tortillas. Cut each tortilla into 6 even-sized triangles.

3 Place the tortilla pieces in the air fryer basket in a single layer – you will have to cook them in batches. Cook each batch for 6-9 minutes until they are crisp and golden, shaking the basket every 2-3 minutes. Remove them and cool them on a wire rack while you cook the remaining batches in the same way.

4 Eat the chips immediately or store them in an airtight container in a cool place for up to 3 days.

★ Tip: Don't worry if the tortilla chips are not super crisp when you take them out of the air dryer – they crisp up as they cool.

VARIATIONS
• Sprinkle the cooked hot tortilla chips with some dried herbs, e.g. oregano.

• Serve with dips, e.g. hummus, blue cheese, tzatziki, black bean.

• Use for making nachos.

SAUSAGE ROLLS

Sausage rolls are the perfect finger food for parties and buffets, but they are also ideal as a snack or even a light lunch served with some salad. Homemade sausage rolls taste so much better than bought ones.

MAKES ABOUT 24 SAUSAGE ROLLS / PREP: 20 MINUTES / COOK: 15-20 MINUTES

450g (1lb) good-quality pork sausage meat
1 onion, grated
2 tsp chopped sage
sea salt and freshly ground black pepper
flour, for dusting
320g (11oz) ready-rolled puff pastry
1 large free-range egg, beaten
tomato ketchup or mustard, to serve

1 Put the sausage meat, onion and sage in a mixing bowl and season the mixture with salt and pepper. Stir until everything is well combined.

2 Lightly flour a clean work surface and lay the pastry sheet on top. Roll it out thinly until you have a large rectangle, then cut it lengthways into 3 long strips.

3 Divide the sausage meat mixture into 3 equal portions and roll and mould them into long cylindrical pieces with your hands. They should be about the same length as the pastry strips.

4 Place a sausage meat cylinder on one of the pastry strips and lightly brush one of the long pastry edges with beaten egg. Fold the pastry over the sausage meat to enclose it and press the pastry edges together to seal them. Turn the long sausage roll over so the sealed edge is underneath.

5 Cut the cylinder into 5cm (2in) long sections to make sausage rolls. Make 2-3 diagonal cuts on top of each and brush them with beaten egg. Repeat with the remaining sausage meat and pastry.

6 Heat the air fryer to 200°C/400°F.

7 Place the sausage rolls in the basket in a single layer with a little space between each – you may have to cook them in batches depending on the size of your air fryer. Cook them for 15–20 minutes, checking on them after 10 minutes, until the pastry is golden brown and the sausage meat thoroughly cooked.

8 Cool the sausage rolls on a wire rack. Serve them warm or cold with ketchup, mustard or a dip of your choice.

VARIATIONS
• Vary the flavourings: try chopped thyme, fennel seeds, chilli flakes, chives or crushed garlic.

• Serve with a honey mustard dip or some spicy tomato chutney.

EASY-PEASY PITTA PIZZAS

These 15-minute pizzas are the ultimate savoury snack or light lunch when you're in a hurry and don't have time to cook. They are delicious, healthy, versatile and use familiar store cupboard ingredients. If you prefer to make your own pizza dough, see box opposite.

SERVES 4 / PREP: 10 MINUTES / COOK: 4-6 MINUTES

4 pitta breads
4 tbsp tinned chopped
    tomatoes, strained
½ tsp dried herbs, e.g.
    marjoram, oregano, thyme
8 stoned (pitted) black olives
125g (4½oz/1¼ cups) grated
    (shredded) mozzarella
spray olive oil
sea salt and freshly ground
    black pepper

TOPPING
fresh basil or rocket (arugula)
    leaves
pesto for drizzling

1   Heat the air fryer to 200°C/400°F.

2   Top the pitta breads with the chopped tomatoes. Spread them out thinly, but leave a border around the edge. Season with salt and pepper.

3   Sprinkle them with the herbs and olives, then scatter the mozzarella over the top. Mist them with a light spray of olive oil.

4   Place two pizzas at a time in the air fryer and cook them for 4-6 minutes until the mozzarella is golden and bubbling and the pitta crust is crisp.

5   Scatter the tops with fresh basil or rocket leaves, or drizzle them with pesto, and serve hot.

VARIATIONS
• Use tomato purée or passata instead of tinned tomatoes.
• Add capers or sliced spring onions (scallions).
• Add roasted or grilled red and yellow (bell) peppers.
• Add diced ham or shredded chicken.
• Top with thinly sliced prosciutto, chorizo or pepperoni.
• Add tinned tuna to make a tuna melt pizza.

MAKE YOUR OWN PIZZA DOUGH

400g (14oz) plain (all-purpose) flour, plus extra for dusting
7g (¼oz/1 sachet) fast-action dried yeast
1 tsp caster (superfine) sugar
1 tsp fine sea salt
2 tbsp olive oil, plus extra for drizzling
225ml (8fl oz/scant 1 cup) water

1 Put the flour, yeast, sugar and salt into a large bowl and make a well in the centre. Pour in the oil and the water and mix well until you have a ball of dough that leaves the sides of the bowl clean.

2 On a lightly floured surface, knead the dough with your hands for 1 minute, or until it is smooth and elastic. Set it aside to rest for 15 minutes.

3 Divide the dough into 2 or 4 equal pieces, depending on the size of your air fryer, and roll them out into circles about 5mm (¼in) thick, but with a slightly thicker border. Spread them with the toppings opposite, then drizzle them with oil.

4 Cook the pizzas in the air fryer at 190°C/375°F for 7-8 minutes.

HONEY MUSTARD ROAST PARSNIPS

These crisp, sweet and golden glazed parsnips make a great accompaniment to casseroles and roasts. They are easy to prepare and cook fast in the air fryer. If you don't have wholegrain mustard, use Dijon instead.

SERVES 4 / PREP: 10 MINUTES / COOK: 15-20 MINUTES

2 tbsp clear honey
1 tbsp olive oil
2 tbsp wholegrain mustard
450g (1lb) thick parsnips
    (3-4 parsnips), peeled and
    cut into 4 lengthwise
sea salt and freshly ground
    black pepper

1 Mix the honey, oil and mustard in a bowl and season with salt and pepper.

2 Turn the parsnip pieces in the honey mustard glaze until they are coated all over.

3 Heat the air fryer to 200°C/400°F.

4 Place the parsnips in the air fryer basket in a single layer (reserving any unused honey mustard mixture) and cook them for 10 minutes, shaking the basket once or twice. Brush them with the leftover glaze and cook them for a further 5-10 minutes, or until they are golden brown and tender.

VARIATIONS
• Cook carrots in the same way.

• Vegans can use maple syrup instead of honey.

• Sprinkle with chopped herbs or chilli flakes.

MOROCCAN ROASTED CARROTS

Carrots roasted in the air fryer are deliciously sweet and tender. These are flavoured with aromatic spices, but you could just use olive oil and drizzle them with honey or honey mustard at the end.

SERVES 4 / PREP: 10 MINUTES / COOK: 12-15 MINUTES

1 tsp za'atar
½ tsp ground cumin
½ tsp ground coriander
2 tbsp olive oil
500g (1lb 2oz) carrots, peeled and sliced in half or quarters lengthways
clear honey, for drizzling
sea salt and freshly ground black pepper
labneh or tahini drizzle (see page 136), to serve (optional)

1   Mix the spices in a bowl with the oil and a good grinding of salt and pepper. Add the carrots and turn them in the oil until they are coated all over.

2   Heat the air fryer to 180°C/350°F.

3   Place the carrots in the air fryer basket in a single layer. Depending on the size of your air fryer, you may need to cook them in batches. Cook them for 10 minutes, shaking the basket once or twice, then drizzle the honey over them and cook them for a further 2–5 minutes, or until they are tender and golden.

4   Serve the carrots with some labneh or drizzled with tahini sauce, if liked.

★ Tip: Labneh is a very thick and creamy cheese made from strained yoghurt, which is often served drizzled with olive oil and sprinkled with herbs or spices.

VARIATIONS
• Instead of honey use maple syrup.
• Vary the spices: try chilli powder, cayenne, paprika, ground cinnamon and ginger.

HASSELBACK BUTTERNUT SQUASH

Butternut squash is an attractive and delicious vegetable served in this way as a side dish with roast chicken, steak, a grain bowl or even pasta. It's great for entertaining when you want to impress your guests.

SERVES 4 / PREP: 15 MINUTES / COOK: 35-40 MINUTES

1 small – about 600g (1lb 5oz) – butternut squash, peeled, halved, lengthways, seeds discarded
spray oil
30g (1oz/2 tbsp) unsalted butter
2 tbsp maple syrup or clear honey
1 tsp chopped sage leaves
sea salt and freshly ground black pepper
crushed dried chilli flakes, for sprinkling

1 Heat the air fryer to 200°C/400°F.

2 Put one squash half cut side down on a chopping board and place a wooden spoon or chopstick on either side of the squash lengthwise. This will stop you cutting right through it.

3 Start at one end and make deep vertical cuts through the squash with a sharp knife, taking care not to cut right through it. The cuts should be approximately 3mm (⅛in) apart. Keep cutting until you reach the other end, and then repeat with the other squash half.

4 Spray the squash halves with oil and season them with salt and pepper. Place them cut-side up in the air fryer basket. Cook them for 20 minutes.

5 While the squash is cooking, heat the butter, maple syrup or honey and sage in a small saucepan over a low heat, stirring until the butter melts.

6 Brush the butter glaze over the squash and cook it for 15–20 minutes more, or until the squash is tender and golden brown. Serve, sprinkled with chilli flakes.

★ Tip: You can remove the skin from the squash with a potato peeler.

VARIATIONS
• Use finely chopped thyme or oregano instead of sage.
• Dust with smoked paprika just before serving.
• Add a dash of balsamic vinegar to the buttery glaze.
• Sprinkle with crispy bacon or crumbled feta cheese.

CAULIFLOWER STEAKS

These cauliflower steaks are surprisingly meaty and filling. Enjoy them as a side dish, an appetizer or even a light meal (see the variations below). Cauliflower packs quite a nutritional punch – it's rich in minerals, fibre and vitamins, especially vitamin C, as well as healthy antioxidants.

SERVES 4 / PREP: 10 MINUTES / COOK: 13-15 MINUTES

1 medium cauliflower, stalk trimmed and leaves removed
2 tbsp olive oil or avocado oil
2 tsp spice seasoning, e.g. Cajun, Mexican, Italian
chopped parsley or coriander (cilantro), for sprinkling
sea salt and freshly ground black pepper

1 Cut the cauliflower in half vertically through the top and the stem. Slice each half into two 2.5cm (1in) thick pieces or steaks. Brush them lightly with oil and sprinkle them evenly with your choice of seasoning – or make your own seasoning (see below).

2 Heat the air fryer to 190°C/375°F.

3 Place the cauliflower steaks in the air fryer basket in a single layer – depending on the size of your air fryer, you may need to cook them in batches. Cook them for 10 minutes, then turn them over and sprinkle them with more seasoning. Cook them for 3–5 minutes more, or until they are crisp and golden brown outside and cooked through.

4 Serve sprinkled with chopped parsley or coriander.

VARIATIONS
• Make your own seasoning by mixing ½ teaspoon each of ground cumin, turmeric or paprika (sweet or smoked) with garlic powder or paste and the oil.

• Mix crushed garlic and chilli flakes with the oil and brush over the cauliflower.

• Serve the steaks as a light lunch with homemade Mediterranean-style tomato sauce and pasta.

• Sprinkle the steaks with finely grated Parmesan.

★ Tip: Test whether the cauliflower is tender by inserting the point of a sharp knife.

PARMESAN AND TRUFFLE CRUNCHY BITES

For truffle lovers, these golden crispy potatoes are as good as it gets. You can also use plain olive oil and sea salt instead and flavour them with your favourite spice mix. They are great to serve with drinks or to eat as an appetizer.

SERVES 4 / PREP: 10 MINUTES / COOK: 20-25 MINUTES

800g (1¾lb) Russet potatoes, scrubbed and cut into 2cm (¾in) cubes
2 tbsp truffle oil
½ tsp sweet paprika or cayenne
1 tsp fine sea salt
2 tbsp grated Parmesan
a few sprigs of flat-leaf parsley, chopped

1 Put the potato cubes in a bowl and add the truffle oil, paprika and salt. Stir until they are lightly coated all over.

2 Heat the air fryer to 190°C/375°F.

3 Place the cubes in the air fryer basket and cook them for 20 minutes, shaking the basket every 5 minutes, until they are tender, crisp and golden. If they are not cooked increase the temperature to 200°C/400°F and cook for 5 minutes more.

4 Tip the potatoes into a large bowl and sprinkle them with Parmesan and parsley. Toss them lightly and season to taste with more salt, if needed. Serve immediately while they are piping hot.

VARIATIONS
• Use Maris Piper potatoes instead of Russets.

• For a more intense truffle flavour, use truffle salt instead of sea salt.

• Add some crushed garlic when you toss the potatoes with the Parmesan.

DESSERTS & BAKES

Here are some straightforward and quick recipes for your favourite puddings without an additive in sight. An air fryer cooks dishes in so little time that you can have a dessert ready in as little as 20 minutes without sacrificing any flavour. You may need to cook some of these dishes in batches, depending on the shape and size of your air fryer. Alternatively, you can simply adjust the ingredient quantities to cook smaller portions for fewer people.

SPICED CARROT CAKE WITH ORANGE FROSTING

This is the easiest carrot cake you'll ever make, and it's really moist and delicious. This recipe uses olive oil rather than butter (to reduce the saturated fat, which makes it healthier) and yoghurt in the frosting. It's very satisfying to know that you can get some vitamin A, C and D plus potassium, phosphorus, magnesium, zinc and calcium from a delicious slice of cake!

SERVES 8 / PREP: 15 MINUTES / COOK: 30-35 MINUTES

175g (6oz/scant 1 cup) light brown sugar
120ml (4fl oz/½ cup) light olive oil
3 medium free-range eggs, beaten
225g (8oz) carrots, grated
grated zest and juice of 1 large orange
175g (6oz/1¾ cups) wholemeal self-raising (self-rising) flour
1 tsp baking powder
1 tsp ground cinnamon
½ tsp grated nutmeg
1 tsp icing (confectioner's) sugar

ORANGE FROSTING
115g (4oz/½ cup) 0% fat Greek yoghurt
115g (4oz/½ cup) light soft cheese
2-3 tbsp icing (confectioner's) sugar
grated zest of 1 orange

★ Tip: Instead of frosting the cake, dust it with icing sugar. It will stay moist and fresh in a tin or airtight container in a cool place for up to 5 days.

1 Lightly oil a 450g (1lb) loaf tin (pan) and line it with baking parchment.

2 Beat the sugar, oil and eggs until they are well blended in a mixing bowl or food mixer. Mix in the grated carrot and orange zest. Sift in the flour and baking powder and mix well. Stir in the spices with most of the orange juice and spoon the mixture into the lined loaf tin. Level the top.

3 Heat the air fryer to 160°C/325°F, having removed the rack if it has one.

4 Place the tin in the air fryer basket and cook the cake for 20 minutes. Cover it with foil and cook for a further 10–15 minutes, or until a skewer inserted into the centre comes out clean. Cool the cake in the tin and then turn it out on to a wire rack.

5 Make the orange frosting: put all the ingredients, plus the leftover orange juice from making the cake, into a bowl and mix them until they are smooth and creamy. Spread the frosting over the top of the cooled cake and decorate it with orange zest. Store the cake in an airtight container in the fridge for up to 3 days.

VARIATIONS
• Add some sultanas (golden raisins) and/or chopped walnuts to the cake mixture.

BANANA BREAD

This is a delicious treat at any time of day: for breakfast, a mid-morning snack, a packed lunch or at teatime. It's very moist and keeps well wrapped in kitchen foil for several days. It also freezes successfully. And it's a great way of using up overripe bananas.

MAKES 1 LOAF / PREP: 15 MINUTES / COOK: 30-40 MINUTES

115g (4oz/½ cup) butter, softened

175g (6oz/¾ cup) caster (superfine) sugar

2 medium free-range eggs

3 ripe bananas, peeled and mashed

75g (3oz/scant ½ cup) chopped walnuts

225g (8oz/generous 2 cups) self-raising (self-rising) flour

½ tsp sea salt

½ tsp grated nutmeg

¼ tsp ground cinnamon

a few drops of vanilla extract

½ tsp bicarbonate of soda (baking soda)

1 Lightly butter a 450g (1lb) loaf tin (pan) and line it with baking parchment.

2 Use a hand-held electric hand whisk to cream the butter and sugar in a mixing bowl. Beat in the eggs, one at a time. Stir in the mashed bananas and nuts, then sift the flour, salt and ground spices into the mixture. Fold them in gently. Finally, fold in the vanilla extract and bicarbonate of soda.

3 Heat the air fryer to 160°C/325°F, having removed the rack if it has one.

4 Transfer the banana mixture to the lined loaf tin and level the top. Place the tin in the basket and cook the loaf for 20 minutes. Check that it's not browning too fast – if it does, cover it with foil or reduce the heat a little. Cook it for a further 10–20 minutes, or until it is golden brown and cooked. Test by inserting a thin skewer into the centre. It's ready when the skewer comes out clean.

5 Leave the banana bread to cool in the tin for 10 minutes before turning it out on to a wire cooling rack. When it is completely cold, slice it and serve it plain or buttered.

★ Tip: Use pure vanilla extract rather than essence, which is artificially made with water, ethanol, emulsifiers and artificial flavours and colourings

VARIATIONS
- Use pecans instead of walnuts.
- Stir in some chocolate chips.

FLAPJACKS

Who doesn't like flapjacks? They're so deliciously sweet, nutty and crunchy. These flapjacks are packed with oats, fruit and nuts, making them high in fibre and full of nutritional goodness. And they have some chocolate chips as a special treat!

MAKES ABOUT 9 FLAPJACKS / PREP: 15 MINUTES / COOK: 15-20 MINUTES

100g (4oz/¼ cup) golden syrup
125g (4½oz/generous ½ cup) light brown sugar
225g (8oz/1 cup) unsalted butter, plus extra for greasing
300g (10oz/3 cups) jumbo oats
a pinch of sea salt
50g (2oz) dried fruit, e.g. cranberries, cherries, raisins
50g (2oz) chopped pecans or walnuts
50g (2oz) dark (bittersweet) chocolate chips

1 Butter a 20 x 20cm (8 x 8in) square cake tin (pan) and line it with baking parchment (see note below). Alternatively, use a foil pan that fits your air fryer.

2 Put the golden syrup, sugar and butter in a saucepan and set it over a medium heat. When the butter melts, stir in the oats, sea salt, dried fruit, nuts and chocolate chips.

3 Transfer the mixture to the lined tin, pressing it into the corners, and smooth the top with the back of a spoon.

4 Heat the air fryer to 160°C/325°F.

5 Place the tin in the air fryer basket and cook it for 15-20 minutes, or until the mixture is golden brown.

6 Take out the tin and set it aside for 1-2 hours, or until the mixture is completely cold and firm. Cut it into squares and store them in an airtight container for up to 5 days.

Note: The tin you use will depend on the size and shape of your air fryer basket. You can cook the flapjack mixture in a square, rectangular or round tin. If your air fryer is quite small, use a smaller tin (17cm/7in) and reduce the quantities accordingly, or cook the flapjacks in two batches.

VARIATIONS
• Use maple syrup or honey instead of golden syrup.
• Add some dried seeds to the flapjack mix.
• Substitute rolled porridge oats for jumbo oats.
• Flavour with grated orange zest or some vanilla extract.

LEMON DRIZZLE CAKE

Loaf cakes are easy to make and speedy to cook in an air fryer. This one has a bright and zingy citrus flavour and a sticky syrup topping – and it stays moist for several days. You'll find it more delicious than the mass-produced cakes in your local supermarket. You also know exactly what is in it – there's no colouring, emulsifiers, preservatives, humectants or palm oil, just familiar ingredients.

SERVES 8-10 / PREP: 15 MINUTES / COOK: 40-45 MINUTES

spray oil
225g (8oz/1 cup) butter, softened
225g (8oz/1 cup) caster (superfine) sugar
3 medium free-range eggs
225g (8oz/generous 2 cups) self-raising (self-rising) flour
grated zest and juice of 1 lemon

SYRUP
juice of 2 lemons
4 tbsp caster (superfine) sugar

1 Lightly spray a 450g (1lb) loaf tin (pan) with oil. Line the tin with baking parchment.

2 Use a food processor or a hand-held electric whisk to beat the butter and sugar until they are creamy, pale and fluffy. Add the eggs one at a time, beating well after each one. Sift the flour into the bowl and beat the mixture well. Finally stir in the grated lemon zest and juice.

3 Preheat the air fryer to 160°C/325°F.

4 Spoon the cake mixture (batter) into the lined loaf tin and level the top. Place the tin in the air fryer basket and cook the cake for 40-45 minutes, or until it is well risen and a skewer inserted in the centre comes out clean.

5 Make the syrup: in a small saucepan set over a low heat, heat the lemon juice and sugar, stirring until the sugar dissolves. Pierce the top of the hot cake several times with a skewer and pour over the warm syrup.

6 Let the cake cool in the tin before removing the paper wrapping. Cut it into slices to serve. The cake will keep well for 4-5 days stored in an airtight container.

⭐ Tip: If the cake mixture is too thick, you can slacken it with 1-2 tablespoons of milk.

VARIATIONS
• Sprinkle the cake with lemon zest.

• Use orange or lime zest and juice instead of lemon.

• Drizzle a little lemon glacé icing over the top and let it drip down the sides of the cake.

BLUEBERRY MUFFINS

Making your own muffins is very satisfying and they taste so much better than bought ones, which may contain ultra-processed ingredients. Baking them in the air fryer saves time too!

MAKES 6 MUFFINS / PREP: 10 MINUTES / COOK: 12-16 MINUTES

50g (2oz/¼ cup) butter, softened

85g (3oz/⅓ cup) caster (superfine) sugar

1 large free-range egg

5 tbsp Greek yoghurt

2 tbsp milk

a few drops of vanilla extract

150g (5oz/1½ cups) self-raising (self-rising) flour

¼ tsp bicarbonate of soda (baking soda)

100g (3½oz/1 cup) blueberries

icing (confectioner's) sugar, for dusting

VARIATIONS

• Substitute raspberries or cranberries for the blueberries.

• Use chocolate chips instead of fruit.

• Add some grated lemon zest to the muffin mixture.

• For a crunchy topping, sprinkle the muffins with demerara sugar before cooking.

1 Line a 6-hole muffin tin (pan) with paper cases (see tip below).

2 Beat the butter and sugar with a hand-held electric whisk until they are light and fluffy. Beat in the egg and then the yoghurt, milk and vanilla extract. Fold in the flour and bicarbonate of soda – the mixture should not be stiff or liquid. If it's too stiff, add a little more milk; if too liquid, add a little flour.

3 Gently fold in the blueberries, distributing them throughout the mixture, and then spoon it into the paper cases.

4 Heat the air fryer to 160°C/325°F.

5 Place the tin in the air fryer basket and cook the muffins for 12–16 minutes, or until they have risen and are golden brown. To test if they are cooked, insert a fine skewer into the centre of one – it should come out clean.

6 Leave the muffins in the tin for a few minutes before cooling them on a wire rack. Serve dusted with icing sugar. The muffins will keep well stored in an airtight container for up to 4 days.

★ Tip: If you don't have a muffin tin or it doesn't fit your air fryer, use silicone muffin cups.

BLACKBERRY AND APPLE CRUMBLE

A fruit crumble is one of the simplest desserts you can make in your air fryer. It might be humble but it's one of the best-loved puddings. When apples are not in season, you can make it with plums, greengages, rhubarb, gooseberries or peaches.

SERVES 4 / PREP: 15 MINUTES / COOK: 25-27 MINUTES

900g (2lb) cooking (green) apples, peeled, cored and cubed
25g (1oz/2 tbsp) light brown sugar
100g (3½oz/1 cup) blackberries
2 tbsp water

NUTTY CRUMBLE
100g (3½oz/½ cup) butter, chilled and chopped, plus extra for greasing
200g (7oz/2 cups) plain (all-purpose) flour
50g (2oz/¼ cup) demerara sugar
25g (1oz/¼ cup) flaked almonds

1 Lightly butter a deep baking dish, cake tin (pan) or foil pan that fits inside the air fryer basket.

2 Put the apples, sugar, blackberries and water in the baking dish and toss them gently.

3 Heat the air fryer to 180°C/350°F.

4 Place the dish in the air fryer basket and cook the fruit for 10 minutes. Stir the mixture and cook it for 5 more minutes, or until the apples are tender.

5 Meanwhile, make the nutty crumble: with your fingertips rub the butter into the flour in a large bowl. When the mixture resembles breadcrumbs, stir in the sugar and nuts. Add 2-3 teaspoons of cold water and stir gently.

6 Cover the fruit mixture with the crumble and cook it for 10-12 minutes, or until the top is crisp and golden brown.

7 Serve the crumble warm with cream, crème fraîche, ice cream, Greek yoghurt or custard.

⭐ Tip: You can make the crumble topping in advance and keep it in the fridge overnight.

VARIATIONS
• Flavour the fruit with ground cinnamon, ginger or cloves.

• Substitute rolled oats for some of the flour in the crumble mixture.

• Use less flour and make up the difference with ground almonds.

ITALIAN BAKED STUFFED PEACHES

Air fryer desserts don't come simpler than this one – it's delicious and decadent, perfect for when you feel like a treat. Make it when peaches are in season and at their best. When they are ripe they are so juicy and sweet that you can leave out the sugar if you prefer.

SERVES 4 / PREP: 10 MINUTES / COOK: 6-12 MINUTES

4 ripe peaches, halved
    and stoned (pitted)
3 tbsp butter, softened
2 tsp light brown sugar
a few drops of almond extract
4 amaretti biscuits, crushed
1 tbsp Amaretto liqueur
    (optional)
maple syrup, for drizzling
Greek yoghurt, mascarpone,
    ice cream or crème fraîche,
    to serve

1   Gently hollow out each peach half a little with a teaspoon to enlarge the stone cavity. Mix the flesh you remove with the butter, sugar, almond extract and crushed amaretti. Fill the peach halves with the amaretti mixture.

2   Heat the air fryer to 180°C/350°F.

3   Line the air fryer basket with some baking parchment and put in the stuffed peach halves, cut-side up, in a single layer. You may have to cook them in two batches depending on the size of the basket. Sprinkle them with Amaretto (if using) and drizzle with maple syrup.

4   Cook the peach halves for 6-12 minutes, checking on them every 2 minutes, or until they are tender, golden brown and starting to caramelize.

5   Serve warm with yoghurt, mascarpone, ice cream or crème fraîche.

VARIATIONS

• Add some ground cinnamon to the stuffing mixture.

• Sprinkle with chopped, flaked or toasted almonds, or crunchy granola.

• Drizzle with honey instead of maple syrup.

BROWNIES

You can eat these squidgy chocolate brownies as a snack or teatime treat, or serve them with whipped cream, crème fraîche or ice cream and fresh raspberries as a delicious dessert. The size of your tin will depend on the size and shape of your air fryer basket. You can cook the brownies in a square, rectangular or round tin or baking dish. If your air fryer is quite small, use a smaller tin, 17cm (7in) square or less, and reduce the quantities accordingly, or cook the brownies in two batches.

MAKES 16 BROWNIES / PREP: 15 MINUTES / COOK: 25-30 MINUTES

200g (7oz) dark (bittersweet) chocolate (70% cocoa solids), broken into pieces
200g (7oz/scant 1 cup) unsalted butter, plus extra for greasing
200g (7oz/scant 1 cup) golden caster (superfine) sugar
3 medium free-range eggs
175g (6oz/1¾ cups) plain (all-purpose) flour, sifted
½ tsp baking powder
¼ tsp sea salt flakes

★ Tip: You can buy air fryer accessories, including cake tins and pizza pans that fit your particular model.

VARIATIONS
• Add some chopped walnuts, pecans or hazelnuts
• Add a few drops of vanilla extract.
• Dust the brownies with cocoa or icing (confectioner's) sugar.

1 Grease and line a 20 x 20cm (8 x 8in) cake tin (pan) with baking parchment.

2 Bring a small saucepan of water to the boil and remove it from the heat. Put the chocolate in a heatproof bowl and suspend it over the pan so the bottom of the bowl doesn't touch the water below. Stir the chocolate occasionally with a flat-bladed knife until it softens and melts.

3 Beat the butter and sugar until they are light and fluffy in a food mixer, or using a hand-held electric whisk. Add the eggs, one at a time, beating well after each one.

4 Use a metal spoon to fold in the melted chocolate in a figure-of-eight motion until the mixture is evenly coloured throughout. Sift in the flour and baking powder and fold in gently with the sea salt.

5 Transfer the mixture to the lined cake tin, pressing it into the corners and levelling the top.

6 Heat the air fryer to 160°C/325°F.

7 Place the tin in the air fryer basket and cook the mixture for 25–35 minutes, or until it is set and has a crust on top. Check whether the brownies are cooked by inserting a thin skewer into the centre – the mixture should be just a little fudgy.

8 Leave to cool in the tin and then cut the mixture into 16 squares. The brownies will keep well stored in an airtight container for up to 5 days.

CHOCOLATE CHIP COOKIES

These cookies are so good! Slightly crisp on the outside and soft and squidgy inside, they are studded with delicious dark chocolate chips – perfect for a snack, a lunchbox or to accompany a cup of tea. You can make the cookie dough in advance and leave it in the fridge to rest for an hour or even overnight.

MAKES 12 COOKIES / PREP: 15 MINUTES / COOK: 5-8 MINUTES

115g (4oz/½ cup) unsalted butter, at room temperature
100g (3½oz/½ cup) light brown sugar
1 large free-range egg, beaten
a few drops of vanilla extract
175g (6oz/1½ cups) plain (all-purpose) flour
½ tsp bicarbonate of soda (baking soda)
150g (5oz/scant 1 cup) dark (bittersweet) chocolate chips
a good pinch of salt

1 Line one or two baking trays (depending on the size of your air fryer basket) with baking parchment. Alternatively, if you have an air fryer rack you can line that with baking parchment.

2 Beat the butter and sugar until they are light and fluffy in a food mixer or with a hand-held electric whisk. Gradually beat in the egg, a little at a time, and then add the vanilla extract, flour, bicarbonate of soda, chocolate chips and the salt. Mix on a low speed until the mixture is the consistency of a soft dough.

3 Divide the dough into 12 pieces and roll each one into a ball. Arrange them on the lined baking trays, spacing them out well, and press down lightly to flatten them.

4 Heat the air fryer to 160°C/325°F.

5 Place the cookies in the air fryer basket – if you use two trays you will need to cook them in batches. Alternatively, place them in a single layer on the lined air fryer rack with plenty of space around them, so they have room to spread, and cook them in batches. Cook them for 5-8 minutes, or until they look cooked and golden.

6 Cool the cookies on a wire rack and store them in an airtight container for up to 5 days.

VARIATIONS

• If you don't have chocolate chips, chop a block of dark chocolate into small pieces.

• You can use white or milk chocolate chips.

SPANISH CINNAMON SUGAR DOUGHNUTS

Spanish doughnuts are called churros and they are usually freshly fried for breakfast and often served with a thick chocolate dipping sauce. In Spain and Mexico they are made with just flour and water, but the mixture for this recipe is enriched with butter and eggs and the doughnuts are served dusted with warm and spicy cinnamon sugar. Air-fried doughnuts are healthier and less greasy than doughnuts deep-fried in oil. Enjoy them for dessert with a chocolate or caramel dipping sauce, as a teatime treat – or for brunch.

SERVES 6 / PREP: 15 MINUTES / CHILL: 30 MINUTES / COOK: 15-20 MINUTES

50g (2oz/¼ cup) butter
240ml (8fl oz/1 cup) water
¼ tsp fine sea salt
100g (3½oz/1 cup) plain (all-purpose) flour
2 large free-range eggs
spray oil

CINNAMON SUGAR COATING
100g (3½oz/scant ½ cup) caster (superfine) sugar
1 tsp ground cinnamon

⭐ Tips: Eat the doughnuts while they are fresh and warm – they do not reheat or keep well. Don't worry if you don't have the right-sized piping nozzle. Any large star-shaped nozzle will be fine.

1 Put the butter, water and salt in a saucepan and bring to the boil. Tip in the flour and cook it, beating all the time, until you have a smooth dough that forms a ball and comes away from the sides of the pan. Remove the pan from the heat and beat in the eggs, one at a time.

2 Spoon the dough into a piping bag fitted with a 2cm (1in) star nozzle and pipe 12cm (5in) lengths on to a baking sheet lined with baking parchment. Chill the piped dough in the fridge for 30 minutes.

3 Heat the air fryer to 180°C/350°F.

4 Line the air fryer basket with baking parchment and put in the dough strips in a single layer, leaving some space around them. You may need to cook them in batches, depending on the size of your air fryer. Spray the strips lightly with oil.

5 Cook the dough strips for 15 minutes and then check them. If they are not golden brown and crisp, cook them for another 5 minutes, checking them every minute or so.

6 Meanwhile, make the cinnamon sugar: mix the sugar and cinnamon in a shallow bowl. Dredge the hot doughnuts with the sugar and serve them immediately.

SURPRISE CUPCAKES

Everyone loves biting into one of these cupcakes and discovering a surprise mini chocolate egg hidden inside. They are easy to make and children will enjoy helping you and cleaning out the bowls!

MAKES 12 CUPCAKES / PREP: 15 MINUTES / COOK: 18-20 MINUTES

150g (5oz/generous ½ cup) unsalted butter
150g (5oz/¾ cup) light brown sugar
3 medium free-range eggs
150g (5oz/1½ cups) self-raising (self-rising) flour
1 tbsp milk
a few drops of vanilla extract
12 mini chocolate eggs

BUTTERCREAM
50g (2oz/¼ cup) butter, softened
75g (3oz/scant ½ cup) icing (confectioner's) sugar, plus extra for dusting
a few drops of vanilla extract
1-2 tsp milk

VARIATION
• You can turn these into 'butterfly cakes' – cut each reserved cone in half to create a pair of wings. Place on top of the cakes and dust with some icing (confectioner's) sugar.

1   Place 12 paper muffin cases in one 12-hole or two 6-hole muffin tins (pans), depending on the size of your air fryer basket.

2   Beat the butter and sugar together until they are creamy, light and fluffy. Beat in the eggs one at a time using a hand-held electric whisk or a food mixer.

3   Sift the flour into the bowl and fold it in gently. Slacken the mixture with the milk and stir in the vanilla extract.

4   Heat the air fryer to 160°C/325°F.

5   Divide the mixture between the paper cases and place them in the air fryer basket – you may have to cook them in batches depending on the size of the basket. Cook them for 18-20 minutes, or until the cupcakes are well risen and a thin skewer inserted into a cake comes out clean. Cool them on a wire rack.

6   While the cupcakes are cooking make the buttercream: beat the butter and icing sugar until they are soft and creamy. Beat in the vanilla extract and milk.

7   Cut a shallow inverted cone out of the centre of each cupcake and place a mini chocolate egg in the hollow. Set aside the cones (see variation). Spoon the buttercream into a piping bag fitted with a star nozzle and pipe a rosette on top of each cupcake to cover the chocolate egg.

8   The cakes will keep well in an airtight container in a cool place for 3-4 days.

CINNAMON BUNS

These spicy, sugary cinnamon rolls aren't just for breakfast or brunch – you can enjoy them at any time of day. Don't be put off by the ingredients list and the time it takes to make them. The recipe is very easy and the hands-on time is less than you think, especially if you have a stand mixer to do the work for you. They cook much faster in an air fryer than in a standard oven and their intoxicating fragrance will fill your kitchen and waft through your home.

MAKES 7-10 BUNS / PREP: 40 MINUTES / RISE: 1 HOUR / PROVE: 45 MINUTES / COOK: 10-20 MINUTES

240ml (8fl oz/1 cup) warm (tepid) milk
50g (2oz/¼ cup) caster (superfine) sugar
1 x 7g (¼oz) sachet easy-blend yeast
1 large free-range egg
85g (3oz/⅓ cup) butter, melted
400g (14oz/4 cups) strong white bread flour, plus extra for sprinkling
1 tsp salt
beaten egg, for glazing
100g (3½oz/generous ¾ cup) icing (confectioner's) sugar
1 tbsp lemon juice or water

CINNAMON FILLING
100g (3½oz/scant ½ cup) unsalted butter, softened
85g (3oz/⅓ cup) light brown sugar
1 tbsp ground cinnamon

1 Put the milk, sugar and yeast in a large bowl and set the mixture aside for 10 minutes, or until bubbles appear and it starts to foam.

2 Beat in the egg and melted butter and then sift in the flour and salt. Mix everything well until you have a sticky dough that comes away from the sides of the bowl.

3 Turn out the dough on to a lightly floured surface and knead it well until it's smooth and elastic. This may take 10 minutes by hand. Alternatively, make the dough in an electric stand mixer and use the dough hook attachment to knead it.

4 Place the ball of dough in a lightly oiled bowl and cover it with cling film (plastic wrap). Set it aside in a warm place for 1 hour, or until the dough is well risen and doubled in size.

5 While the dough is rising, mix all the ingredients for the cinnamon filling.

VARIATIONS

• Add some grated lemon or lime zest to the icing.

• You can bake the buns in a tin that fits inside your air fryer.

6   Place the risen dough on a clean floured surface and roll it out into a rectangle about 1cm (½in) thick. Spread the cinnamon filling over the dough and then roll it up into a long cylinder, starting from one of the long sides. Slice the roll into 8–10 pieces and place them, spiral-side up, on a baking tray lined with baking parchment. Cover the slices with baking parchment or a clean tea towel and leave them for 45 minutes, or until they double in size.

7   Heat the air fryer to 180°C/350°F. Line the basket with baking parchment.

8   To glaze the buns, brush them lightly with beaten egg and then place them in a single layer in the air fryer basket with a little space between them. You may have to cook them in batches, depending on the size of your air fryer. Cook the buns for 10–20 minutes, checking them often after the first 5 minutes to ensure that they do not go too brown. If they seem to be browning too fast, cover them with baking parchment or kitchen foil. They are ready when they are cooked through and golden brown. Cool them on a wire rack while you make the glacé icing (frosting).

9   Sift the icing sugar into a bowl and gradually stir in the lemon juice or water until you have a smooth and glossy mixture. If it's too thick, add more liquid; too thin, add more sugar.

10   Drizzle the icing over the cooled buns and serve. They will keep well in an airtight container in the fridge for up to 3 days.

HOMEMADE BREAD

Breadmaking is soothing and satisfying, even though it is quite a lengthy process as the dough needs time to rise and prove. You can bake a small – 450g (1lb) – loaf in your air fryer. Remember that air fryer models vary in size and power, so you will need to check on the loaf regularly after 20 minutes and adjust the timing if necessary.

MAKES 1 450G (1LB) LOAF / PREP: 25 MINUTES / RISE: 1 HOUR / PROVE: 45 MINUTES / COOK: 25-35 MINUTES

250g (9oz/2½ cups) strong white bread flour
¾ tsp fine sea salt
1 tsp sugar
1 x 7g (¼oz) sachet easy-blend yeast
2 tbsp milk
90ml (3fl oz/scant ½ cup) water
1 tbsp melted butter
milk or beaten egg, to glaze

1   Sift the flour and salt into a large mixing bowl. Stir in the sugar and yeast.

2   Heat the milk and water until they are hand-hot, then mix them into the flour with the melted butter to form a soft dough.

3   Turn the dough out on to a lightly floured surface and knead it for 10 minutes until it's elastic and smooth. Transfer it to a lightly oiled bowl and leave it to rise in a warm place for 1 hour, or until it has doubled in size.

4   Knock the dough down with your fists and shape it into a loaf. Place it in a lightly oiled 450g (1lb) loaf tin (pan). Cover it with a clean tea towel and leave the dough in a warm place for 45 minutes, or until the dough has risen to almost fill the tin.

5   Heat the air fryer to 200°C/400°F.

6   Lightly brush the top of the loaf with milk or beaten egg and place it in the air fryer basket. Cook it for 20–25 minutes, or until it is risen and golden brown. Remove the loaf from the tin and place it in the air fryer basket. Cook it for 5–10 more minutes until it's cooked underneath and it sounds hollow when you tap the base with your knuckles.

⭐ Tip: You can make the bread in a food mixer fitted with a dough hook if you don't want the work of kneading it by hand.

7   Cool the loaf on a wire rack and slice it to serve. It will stay fresh in a bread bin or wrapped in foil or plastic in a cool place (not the fridge) for 3–4 days.

INDEX

HarperCollins*Publishers*
1 London Bridge Street
London SE1 9GF

www.harpercollins.co.uk

HarperCollins*Publishers*
Macken House, 39/40 Mayor Street Upper
Dublin 1, D01 C9W8, Ireland

First published by HarperCollins*Publishers* 2024

10 9 8 7 6 5 4 3 2 1

A catalogue record of this book is available from the British Library

ISBN 978-0-00-868504-1

Recipes: Heather Thomas
Photography: Sophie Fox
Food Styling: Pippa Leon
Prop Styling: Faye Wears

Printed and bound in Bosnia-Herzegovina

WHEN USING KITCHEN APPLIANCES PLEASE ALWAYS FOLLOW THE MANUFACTURER'S INSTRUCTIONS